A DP
(DISPLACED PERSON)
FINDS
AMERICAN
DREAM

VALENTINE L. KRUMPLIS

Order this book online at www.trafford.com
or email orders@trafford.com

Most Trafford titles are also available at major online book retailers.

Printed in the United States of America.

ISBN: 978-1-4907-1301-4 (sc)
ISBN: 978-1-4907-1300-7 (e)

Trafford rev. 10/25/2013

 www.trafford.com

North America & international
toll-free: 1 888 232 4444 (USA & Canada)
fax: 812 355 4082

Contents

His Story—Leaving Lithuania

I WAS JUST BEGINNING to develop a memory in September-October 1944 when my world flipped upside down. I do not remember packing or getting loaded in the horse drawn wagon. From the stories of our exodus from Lithuania, I have to take my parents word for it. I seem to remember only fragments of our exodus. We left our beloved land with two horse drawn wagons. Grandpa was in one of them and we were in the other one. It is also interesting that in all the later years no one mentioned the fact that there was a different version of our leaving Lithuania. According to aunt Ona we left with an auto and a truck and she only told me that story when she found out I was looking for fragments of our exodus story.

As we were leaving Lithuania toward Prussia we stopped to say hello to some relatives that lived in a town called Tituvenai. Here the relatives and our group decided to have a big roast goose dinner. After the goose was cooked and placed on a table outside, I was assigned to guard the goose. Well as the parents relate the story, I failed. There were pigs running around in the yard and it seems one of the pigs chased me away and ate the goose. I do not blame myself. I was smaller than the damn pig and they had not given me a weapon to guard the goose. We left without the goose dinner but I think they gave us some smoked hams.

My mother, father, and me, notice my cool haircut

My father was in the Lithuanian Army, sitting on the left.

It rained a lot and the roads got muddy as I remember. Why did we not use the paved roads? The wagons moved in a large endless procession of wagons, carts, bicycles, pedestrians, broken German army units. Sometimes certain army units had to flee faster so they forced the rest of the caravan off the road. During this mess the Russian and German artillery exchanged salvos. We always heard the bursting shells. When things got very hot we left the road and hid in the muddy fields.

Every bridge we came to was mined and ready to be blown up. At one of the bridges grandpa made up his mind to turn around and go back to his farm, he did not want to leave Lithuania. He started back but the rest of the family chased him down and persuaded him to go with us. The soldiers on the bridge were ready to set off the mines and grandpa was one of the last people to cross that bridge. I guess the Russian army was very close on our tail.

My mother tells me she tried to help the war effort by telling the soldiers marching next to us to turn around and go to stop the advancing red army. She failed to even persuade one soldier. She tells me they told her "We are going ZU MUTTI". How can you convince someone to fight when they tell you they are going to their mama?

I think I was dressed too warm, this was February 1943 in Kaunas

I was dressed to travel.

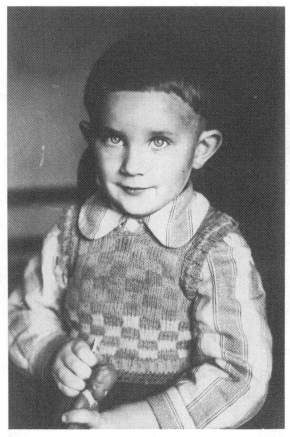

I had my one toy, a doll ? My ears grew faster than my
head at this time

My father's chauffeur driven Mercedes. I am on the fender with my nanny, father is standing with mother, two in center.

Things along the road got progressively worse. It seems the German high command had plans to stop the red advance by digging trenches in the fields and forcing their soldiers to fight. The Germans did not want to dig trenches when there were sixty thousand Lithuanians on the roads to Germany. The German army forced Lithuanian men from the exodus caravans to go dig trenches in the muddy fields. The men left their wives, children, old parents, sick people and were forced to dig holes in the ground while the artillery was getting ever closer. Some people from this forced conscription were never reunited.

Our little family group was lucky. My father had official German documents allowing him to travel all over to buy and inventory grain for the Lietukis Cooperative. He also had permission to have an assistant, grandpa. The Germans were fixated on stamped documents no matter how out of place or stupid they seemed. Here we are in a convoy of thousands of refugees fleeing to Germany with our wagons and horses and the documents say my dad is buying up, or checking the grain harvest. So, my dad, and grandpa got away from digging ditches. I wonder what my dad did with the documents that saved him, and grandpa? The soldiers went from wagon to wagon pulling off all the able bodied men. I would guess if you were fifteen and not over eighty you could dig. We had one other man with us and he was the young husband of my mother's sister Ona. He had no documents and so I was given the task of saving him. Imagine only a little over four years of age and a hero. His name was Ksaveras and my parents hid him under a pile of horse feed, hay, I guess. I was instructed to sit on top of the hay and when the soldiers approached the wagon I was to start crying, screaming, and thrashing about. The soldiers peeked in and were told I was very sick. They did not want to search the wagon.

Bridges were blowing up, artillery shells falling all over and guess what happened in the whole mess . . . a gigantic traffic jam. The convoy ground to a halt. My parents hearing the closeness of the artillery decided that they were better off walking than sitting in the traffic jam. We left Ona and Ksaveras and grandpa and started walking toward Germany. We walked at night on the road and in the fields sometimes. I could not walk very well in my super warm clothes and boots so my poor dad carried me. I never thanked him. I was dead weight, I was not a fat kid but I was heavy. Out of the fields and back on the road the traffic was now moving a little and my dad was huffing and puffing.

Then a miracle happened right there on this one spot on the road, an evil Nazi officer in his carriage had his driver stop by my dad. This evil man, as we portray them today, felt sorry for my dad as he saw him stumbling along carrying this heavy load. He was our good, Samaritan. He offered to put me in the carriage next to him and my parents could walk next to the carriage. The officer explained to my dad that he was paralyzed from the waist down and was going back home to a hospital. He covered me up with the blanket and I sat next to him for a while as we kept traveling to Germany. We should always know that kindness and mercy are not some characteristics of some exclusive nationality or religion.

How my parents and me, met up with the two wagons remains a mystery to me, but we were together again. As the wagons creaked along the road we stopped to rest. We pulled off the road next to a fairly wide creek to cook some food and rest. The road was jammed up again. If a wagon breaks down it takes a while to transfer the people and some goods before it is pushed of the road into a ditch. You can understand the anguish of some wagon owner having to leave all he owns, releasing the horses, and start walking with some bag on his back. The traffic had come to a stop and the road was blocked up. We were heating up some food and my dad saw a small encampment of soldiers, a mobile divisional headquarters. Dad spoke fluent German and went to ask them about the front. Mother should have told him and saved the walk for him. Hey dad, the Germans are running, going to "mutti", what don't you understand?

Meanwhile back in our camp we almost had our first casualty. The traffic on the road was so bad that a German Motorcycle company decided to get off the road and drive through the fields. They drove up to the creek and could not cross it. They saw us and came over to ask to use our horses to get across the creek. Ksaveras who spoke no German believed they wanted to take our horses for good. He was a stubborn man and argued with them. Stupid I thought. The Germans were going to do what they did best, option B, when talking fails, they were going to shoot Ksaveras and use the horses. Another miracle occurred at this time, my dad returned, in time, to talk to the German officer, loan him the horses, and help the motorcycles across the creek. We celebrated that evening, Ksaveras was alive, we had our horses, and my dad had information important to him . . . he was told the German army was retreating. Well we decided to keep going to Germany in that great mass of humanity. There were about sixty thousand Lithuanians escaping the coming liberation of Lithuania. It was far better to leave everything and avoid the communist, Russian liberation. You have to wonder that such an exodus of innocent people was not noticed by the British and American governments. The Lithuanian people were better off in bombed out Germany as displaced people than waiting in their own country for liberation from the evil Nazis.

Mud and more mud, rain and more rain were our constant companions on this muddy road. Wet, cold, and miserable, we decided to pull over and set up camp. I was my mother's main concern. I had developed the sniffles and a runny nose. Mother wanted to put me in a dry and warm place but there were no inns around or hotels except a few farm houses scattered along the road. Mother and Ona spotted a light in a house nearby, and took me with them to see if perhaps the farmer would give us a dry warm corner to spend the night. I was tired and not a happy child. The farm house we approached was filled with German soldiers, inside and outside there were German soldiers. Mother and Ona looked stupid coming into a German army camp, dragging a whining, wet kid. They were also cold, wet, muddy and tired. They knocked on the door and as the door swung open they pushed me into the room and closed the door. There I was in a room full of soldiers, a warm stove, and a dry room. I was four years and four months old and spoke no German. I should have saluted them, but I think I did not.

I was not crying anymore I was too scarred. The soldiers maybe thought I was a new recruit. Hitler was allowing fourteen year olds to fight. Why not four year olds? They took of my wet coat and gave me a blanket. They gave me some warm food to eat. They attempted to talk to me and joke with me. They were wonderful young men caught in the eye of the hurricane and for that one moment perhaps I reminded them of their humanity, their families, and homes. I lucked out and dried out, and was fed. I then began to preach to them, (just joking). I did no such thing. It would have been cute, you have to admit, but I was not that clever . . . yet. Our luck continued because the soldiers decided that my mother and aunt should also keep me company. They were invited in to dry out also and were given some food. We spent the night being dry and warm. I wish I would have learned the names of the soldiers or at least the name of the unit they belonged to.

The next day, we were back on the wagons and the glutted up road. The artillery seemed further back now as we were traveling through what was Prussia. The poor, pathetic, German farmers seeing this exodus of the most miserable people running for their lives through their country had to wonder what type of hell was coming their way. Hell was on the way and brought them murder, rape, torture and all the other great gifts the communists dispensed. A Russian Communist ideologue Illia Ehernberg, a Jew, preached to the troops to kill and rape all the German people.

We finally reached a railway center that connected to the different German cities. There were signs pointing to all different directions and names, but I could not read yet and so can not tell you where we were.

Leaving our wagons, our horses and a lot of our stuff was heart breaking for the family. We traded or sold our horses practically for nothing and that was very painful for grandpa. We packed our stuff into boxes, suitcases and empty bags of horse feed. I believe we had smoked hams, bacon, flour, and home made moonshine. This was food to sustain us and could be used for barter. The problem now was to get on some train, buy some tickets, and figure out where to go. We decided to go as far as we can into Germany to get away from the communist liberators as far as possible. I think our family, even my dad, were beginning to think that the German army was not doing a strategic retreat but were actually running for their lives. While everyone was running around the railroad station I was assigned guard duty of our stuff one more time. I guess the goose incident was forgotten.

We got our tickets and started to look for some empty seats on the train. There were private compartments in some of the wagons and family groups occupied them. Other compartments were being held by a few people who were waiting for the rest of their group to show up.

Dragging our belongings along the train we spotted an almost empty compartment with only two

Latvian men barring the door. They would not let us in. My dad was not a pugilist nor was Ksaveras so we waited for a miracle to occur, I guess. Again a miracle occurred in the shape of two young powerful Lithuanian men. They were Jurgis and Stepas Jakuciai. They wanted also to get on the train but spoke no German and had no idea where to go. We made friends right away by the almost empty compartment. That contact and friendship lasted all of our lives. We were friends forever. They forced the door open into the compartment, shoved the two men aside and helped us aboard the train. The two selfish men were Latvians and I believe they left the compartment. We were on our way into evil, Nazi Germany, getting further away from the liberating communists.

Leaving Lithuania-Ona Information

Lietukis co-operative building in Kaunas. My father was
a director of the grain department and had documents to
check grain production. The documents saved him from
having to dig trenches in Prussia as we were fleeing from
the liberating Russian communist hordes.

O NA GAVE ME an earful on Jan, 27, 2010.
She told me that in Lithuania my family
lived on Prusu Street in a three flat building in
Kaunas. I remember that building little bit. She also
told me that originally my parents and I planned to
leave Lithuania with an auto, a Mercedes, chauffeur
driven, and a truck with some of our stuff. Our maid
Marijona also traveled with us. Ona went on to relate
how our group was stopped by a German patrol and
our two vehicles were confiscated. I had never heard
this version before. My dad always had a chauffeur
driven Mercedes as a director of Lietukis so I can
believe this version of Ona.

We were left with our stuff by the side of the
road as the Germans took our vehicles. Meanwhile
grandpa, Ona, Ona's husband, Ksaveras and another
maid Karuse were traveling with two wagons and
four horses. My parents got a farmer to transport
them to a town called Sakiai where they got in touch
with grandpa and Ona to get them another wagon and
horses. Ona and grandpa were at this time in a city
called Siauliai.

The Germans were grabbing up men and horses
for their war effort, mainly to dig trenches, and so
Ona took one old limping horse and a wagon and
went to get us in Sakiai. We were finally together
and proceeded west to get away from our liberators.
We stopped at Ksavera's home to see his parents and
rest. This was in Suvalkija area. We then proceeded
with the wagons to Germany. In Prusia, Marienburg,
We sold our horses to a German farmer and Grandpa

cried and horses cried according to Ona. She also related another incedent that shows I was nearsighted even back then. We got out of the wagons to walk along side of them and I spotted some cranberry type fruit growing on some stumps along the road. I went to pick them but Ona grabbed me back because she saw several snakes on the stumps. I had not seen them.

In Germany we were assigned where there was work and housing. My parents, and grandpa were sent to Ilsfeld. Ona, Ksaveras, Karusc were sent to a large town to work in an airplane factory. The city was called Ludviksburg, it was close to Ilsfeld.

First Stop In Germany . . . Ilsfeld

TRAIN RIDES AND transfers at bombed out stations in bombed out cities. Always, the air raids and the running for shelters. Always tired, sleepy, dragging bundles of our stuff, we finally arrive at our designated or selected destination . . . Ilsfeld, a small town in the farm country. The interesting thing to me is that amid the bombings the Germans remained organized. You felt safe from looting, murder, robbery, and rape. Why is that? Law and order existed to the very end. I guess it is the cultural and racial characteristic of the European that enforces a certain ethical behavior. This behavior is surely lacking in many other places and races.

After we arrived we were given ration cards, assigned a place to live, and father was given a job at the railroad station. This was in late fall of 1944. I was almost four and a half. I was too young to join the Hitler Jugend, that is why they did not ask me. Also my age was a problem because my mother made me out one year younger in order to get a larger ration of milk. Our documents were bombed out so it was not hard to create new ones. This age thing was not corrected until I was a real sixty five and wanted my social security. My wife Sylvia was surprised when she discovered she was married to an older man. My aunt Jane in Lithuania was amazed when I told her I was born on June 22, 1941. She said she already remembers me running around in May-June 1941 as she was dragged of to Siberia on June 15, 1941. So in her mind I could not have been born seven days after she was deported.

Ilsfeld had a main street and a few stores, a restaurant-beer hall, one railroad station, some closed warehouse or factory buildings. Hitler's secret wonder weapons to win the war were obviously made some where else. We heard about them on the radio constantly. The streets were paved, there were no cars running around that I can remember. The little town was built around the one main street. A hundred yards to each side you were in the farm fields.

My parents and I, and grandpa were assigned to live in a house owned by a little old lady, a spinster, her name was Nana. I do not think she was a dirty Nazi. Her house was a two story cement, brick type little building. The foundations long ago stopped supporting the building and it sagged in many places, like Nana. Nana had the house filled with mementos, doilies, and all kinds of knick knacks. She must have been horrified at our intrusion. Her beliefs were that we would steal, break, and infest her house with lice, fleas and dirt. Poor Nana, It took a while to realize that we were good honest, clean people. She started relaxing and maybe liked grandpa. She also started to give me an egg to eat on certain days when the chickens were not scarred to lay eggs.

I do not know what part of town Ksaveras and my aunt Ona lived. We visited often between the bombings. Life began to normalize, we unpacked, did laundry. Dad went of to work at the railroad station and came back to tell us stories of whole trains of stuff being stuck in town because either the tracks or destinations had been bombed out. Guess what, the stuff was stored and documented and not stolen or pilfered.

In the evenings dad and grandpa would meet fellow Lithuanians in a restaurant for a beer and discussion of world events. No one in their wildest dreams believed that Roosevelt and Churchill would sell out half of Europe to the murdering communist Russians. We believed we would be free and could go back to Lithuania.

My life also got better. I was not being dragged all over Germany and could now get on with being a little kid. Things got really good, I made a friend who lived close by. His name was Helmut Muller, he was slightly older but we got on well and I learned German. I wonder why he did not learn Lithuanian? Helmut would say something and if I did not understand it, then I would ask dad or mother. One phrase I remember was that he told me he must leave for a moment to make a "hoifelle". Mother explained that meant he had to do number two in the bathroom.

I went back to Germany in 1986 and went to Ilsfeld. I found the restaurant and stopped in to have coffee and ask if anyone remembers the Lithuanian people in the town during the war. I spoke in broken German and got across the fact that I lived in Nana's house and had a friend called Helmut. They told me that the reason I could not find Nana's house was that it was demolished long ago. They knew that my friend Helmut was Helmut Muller and called him on the phone to tell him that his little friend during the war was now looking for him. Helmut said he would come right over and as we sat waiting for him the owner of the restaurant and old lady sat down and asked me about my parents, aunt Ona, Ksaveras, grandpa. She remembered all the Lithuanians who stayed in town during the war. She showed me the booth my father sat in and drank beer with his friends. It was amazing to me that I had traveled back in time over forty years and could connect with people that we interacted that long ago. It seemed to me that this town was magical to have such a window into the past. Anyway after some conversation Helmut came into the restaurant and we had our little reunion. My German was coming back to me during that vacation, and I could get my ideas across. Helmut asked us to fallow his car to his farm where he showed us that he was in the diary business. We spent some time talking about our past and the fantastic event of meeting each other forty years later. Helmut also was complaining about the Chernoble explosion which polluted the grass in Germany and he was stopped from selling milk. This was 1986.

Having met Helmut and his whole family brought back a more detailed picture of those last months of the war. I remember almost always at night mother waking me up and dressing me haphazardly while the sirens wailed. Then, half running half being dragged or carried running for the fields, laying down in the wet grass or snow and mother trying to cover me with her body. I wanted to look up into the sky but I think she believed it was dangerous to look. You could now hear the bombers overhead. Sometimes you could see them, hundreds of them. The sky was covered with them from one edge to the other, all you saw was bombers. The droning, the noise they made is unforgettable, a one combined groan like hum, loud and deep. When they flew over, sometimes dropping a bomb here or there to just show us that we are not ignored. There were not many bombs dropped on us. One bomb did drop in Nana's yard and blew up an old well. Grandpa was always late in running for the fields, I guess he was making his bed or something, so on the day of Nana's yard bomb he had just left the area when the well was blown up and all the windows were blown out. I think after this close call for him, he was faster to get to the fields. The all clear sounded and we walked back to the house. One other bomb I remember had fallen into the middle of town but had not exploded. It just sat there like an alien spaceship. Grandpa and I took walks and he would point out the bomb and joke that someone should sit on it and hit the tip with a hammer. I always thought it was a weird thing to say.

The bombers had other interesting things they did besides dropping bombs, they dropped thousands of strips of foil. The foil was a few feet long and a few inches wide and came down all over the fields. We collected these strips and played with them. The foil was dropped to fool the German radar I was told.

The one other thing that I remember was the carpet bombing of some large city close by that lit up the night in our town and you could read the paper at night. I wonder if the Germans had won the war, who would have been hung for war crimes for bombing residential neighborhoods.

There was not much to do in the fields once the bombers left and we were waiting for the all clear. I remember there were old farm building foundations all overgrown with moss. These foundations were the home of hundreds of huge snails with large shells. They were grey in color and had little horns. I would pop them off the cement and line them up. They were fun to watch as they moved around. You can understand that kids at that time did not have a lot of toys so snail watching was cool.

There were some incidents that maybe should have traumatized me, but they did not. I was in the front yard by myself when I saw a policeman going down the street, I think a policeman, he had on a uniform. A large German shepherd dog ran up to him and started trying to bite him. He tried to scare the dog away, but when the dog kept after him he took out his pistol and shot him. I reported this to my mother but she just calmed me down and nothing was said or done about this.

The other thing that was unpleasant was that there was a crippled Nazi living close by and would make remarks about us "auslanders" eating up their resources when all were needed to fight the war. I believe he was the last of the Germans to still believe in Hitler's wonder weapons.

We had brought a lot of stuff from Lithuania and we had a taste for some good bacon and ham. The ration cards toward the end of the war were not all that good and our small family group was forced into crime. Black market was around and we found a farmer who wanted to trade a pig for some of our stuff. I believe we walked the pig into the house were aunt Ona lived. We took the pig to the basement and sealed up the windows. Grandpa was the man assigned to kill the poor pig and we were all in the basement there to help with the processing. We had a large tub of boiling water I guess to shave the pig after it was killed. I am not sure why the water was there. Anyway to make the story short grandpa stabs or cuts the pig, the pig falls down and is carried by the men to the tub and placed in the hot water. The pig revives and leaps out of the water and runs around the basement squealing and splattering blood, almost a perfect crime and now this. I do not remember if the pig died by itself or was stabbed again. Anyway we were not apprehended and had a lot of good food. We also hindered the German war effort by this.

My dad was beginning to be convinced that it was more than a strategic withdrawal by the German army. The old Germans in town led by the Nazi leaders began to organize the "volkstrom", peoples army, a militia of older men to fight in every town.

They went out in force to meet the American unit coming across the fields. The Americans did not want to fire at the town so they stopped at the drainage ditch to see if anyone will surrender the town. The German militia thinking that the ditch was an obstacle fired a shot at the Americans. Ooops, a big mistake, the tanks and troops, jeeps, and trucks roared across the ditch and our town militia threw down their guns. It was over in seconds and now the huge convoy of machines drove through town. Helmut and I stood in the front yard and stared wide eyed at the men and machines. The strange thing that happened was that the soldiers were waiving and laughing. They were not scary at all. We waved back at them and smiled. They started to throw chocolate bars at us and we started to wave some more. My first Hershey with almonds tasted so good.

When Germany was occupied and the war ended we left Ilsfeld and were concentrated in Oberlenningen in the American zone. I never saw or heard from Helmut until 1986 when I visited. We then wrote to each other for a while and then one day I got a letter from his wife that Helmut had died of stomach cancer. Maybe he drank that polluted milk from the reactor explosion in Russia. Today I just have memories of that strange time in Ilsfeld and miss my little friend Helmut Muller. Is he making a "hoifelle" and is gone for the moment only? Now I just treasure the Christmas cards I get from Helmut's family.

To the end of days I will always be grateful to the kind, German people, of Ilsfeld who gave us food, shelter, jobs and treated us as human beings while their own country was being destroyed.

American occupation . . .
we move to Oberlenningen

In Oberlenningen we are sledding down the hill to the cafeteria, my father is holding me in my white outfit.

Oberlenningen

THE AMERICANS CAME in and started organizing the so called displaced persons. We became known as DP's. There were thousands of DP's, liberated arms workers, prisoners, and mixed escapees from the Russian zone. Everyone was looking for lost relatives. The Americans started to move us to special centers so we could be taken care off or repatriated. We ended up in a small town called Oberlenningen. We settled down and started living without any sirens or bombs. The Americans set up a cafeteria for us in a town hall, in the town center. We had to go there for different meals at set times. We lived in a German owned house on a hill. The street led down the hill right to the town hall. I remember this because during our first winter there, my dad and I would ride a sled down the hill and end up at the town hall. Oh what fun it is to ride with a no horse sled with your dad.

I do not remember much interesting happening in this town except that we had to go eat in this large hall. I was a normal eater and ate what the Americans gave us, powdered eggs, powdered milk, oatmeal, farina. I had no problems with the food but there were two brothers and their father who always had a screaming session as the father tried to force feed the young boys. To this day I can not forget the kids spitting out the oatmeal or farina on the table as the father put them in headlocks and tried to shove the food down their throats. The kids were about my age and live in Chicago. I should ask them if they eat farina or oatmeal today.

Like I mentioned before I must have been bored in that town because I do not remember any thing interesting happening to me there. I did have a sixteen year old German girl that was my babysitter. You might ask . . . how do I remember that and her age? Well she told me herself when I visited Germany in 1986 with my wife. It was again like in the Twilight Zone that the memories came back. We drove into the town and I found the hill and the building at the bottom of the hill. I estimated where the hill leveled of at the top and remembered the starting point for our sleigh ride. There was the house and an older lady washing windows on the outside of the house. Stopping the car we got out and I approached the house, the woman stopped working and came to the street, I stammered in my broken German that I had lived here in one of these houses right after the war and that my name is Valentinas Krumplis. A small size miracle occurred at the moment. The woman kept saying "ya", "Krumplis familija lebt in diese house." Anyway something like this, my German was never good or accurate so you have to sort of guess what is being said. She told us that my family lived here and that she would show us the room in the house which we lived in. We went inside and the room was large and in front of the house. Very sunny and very clean and she began to tell us she was sixteen in 1945. She also told me she was sometimes my babysitter. We discussed my parents and other people she remembered. The visit ended with us exchanging addresses and saying so long. We are funny creatures, we do not see someone for forty years and yet there is not much to say when you do see that person. We sent each other Christmas cards and she sent me a German cookbook. She died of some cancer in the nineties and her kids sent me the news. Today I still send Christmas cards to the family, they send me cards also. Somehow that contact keeps your past together. Like a film strip of a movie or an anchor line to your past.

The internment camp-our arrival in Schwabisch Gmund

Me in Schwabisch Gmund

Our family in Schwabisch Gmund. Left to right, mother,
me, father, grandpa, aunt Ona, Ksaveras.

WHAT A NAME. We arrived, I guess
by train at the request of the American
army. This was one way the occupation forces could
figure out how to resettle us or distribute us in some
sensible manner. We were settled in old German
army barracks. The German army did not need them
anymore because most of them were dead, wounded
or serving time in the communist paradise of Siberia.
We were brought into the barracks in great numbers
so choices were limited on who you bunked with. I
guess I was about seven at that time. We were led in
to a large attic hall with beds along the walls and in
the center. Row after row of beds with thick round
white mattresses filled with straw, metal army beds.
Well I think I cried then because my mother and I

could not get two beds side by side. Once again we met an asshole youngish man who would not trade beds and allow my mother to sleep next to me. For some reason I remember him being Latvian. My mother ended up sleeping some fifty beds away from me. Father I do not know where he got to sleep. He was probably trying to get information on German battle lines. This sad episode lasted for a short time and we were able to then get a small private room in the attic. My dad now got a job as translator for the American administration, maybe that is how we got a room. The Americans had their hands full, no one hardly spoke any English, black market was rampant, Nazi collaborators were among us, SS men from volunteer Lithuanians were mixed with us. We also had our problems when we got settled in.

Bedbugs by the millions soon attacked us. I always wondered how the dirty Russians managed to do this to us. I blamed everything on the Russians. It was an easy explanation. Not only millions of bedbugs but also thousands of rats infested our old army compound. There was only one bright light in our lives, there were no Russian communist liberators in camp. Sixty years later I can still remember the smell of DDT powder. The Americans had tons of this DDT powder and they were generous with it. They sprayed us as we lined up, they sprayed our underpants, bras, and all we owned. There was so much white powder in the air that a white out was declared, just joking. But we got sprayed again and again and the bedbugs died by the millions. We defended ourselves against bedbugs in our beds by cleaning and spraying the beds and mattresses. The mattresses smelled of DDT forever, but we knew that it meant we were safe from the little Russian critters. Our top engineers figured out that if we placed pots of water under the legs of beds the bedbugs could not get into our beds, but bedbug engineers figured out that all they had to do to get our blood was to walk on the ceiling and drop on the bed, so we kept spraying.

The rat holocaust was a sight to see. Hundreds of Lithuanians lined up with sticks, shovels, brooms, outside some large storage building and then the brave volunteers would go in and move stuff out and the rats would start running between the people. Lot of rats got killed and everyone felt much better.

My dad continued his work as translator and then he worked for UNRA, a relief agency bringing us clothes and stuff. Dad tells of an interesting story as the interrogations went on by the Americans. People knew that their experiences and education levels would help them get to America or some other place, so they were nervous before the American questioning. The women would get confused and when asked when their last period was, and they gave stupid answers, well dad always saved them by making proper answers. My favorite story was when a loud woman began to tell that she was a masseuse, pedicurist, manicurist, and in her broken speech the American understood prostitute and put that down. I do not know if my dad tried to correct that one.

The gates into our compound were always guarded by two policemen who searched the coming and going of all the people. They looked in the bags for contraband. We had a lot of rules to follow. People were desperate to eat better and to get things that were fun to have, like cigarettes. The Americans were always there smoking like crazy and throwing down their unfinished cigarettes. My grandpa and his gang of smokers were always there to pick up all the butts. There were no filters at that time so there was more tobacco. Cancer was not figured into smoking at that time so a lot of people smoked. No one had time to die of cancer. People were blown up, shot, starved, or sent to Siberia. Anyway at the end of the day the smokers got together with all the butts and sat around a table making a huge mountain of tobacco from the butts. They had some well engineered cigarette making machines and produced bunches of nice looking cigarettes.

Rumors flew around how home made moonshine would kill or blind dozens of people. People wanted to get drunk and so took chances on the home made stuff. The other rumors were that sausages were produced from human meat. This always scarred the kids. We envisioned a person enters a butcher shop, and a trap door in the floor opens and he falls into the basement and is made into a sausage.

We all smelled like DDT but we prospered with the black market. We began to raise chickens, geese, pigs, cows, right in camp under the American noses. This was against all the rules but I think the

Americans were so super nice that most of the time they simply refused to see all the critters hid all over the place. Once in a while some asshole officer decided to see what the hell was going on and started searches. This was the funniest episode as the people scrambled to hide their livestock. One incident stands out the best, is of some Lithuanians, who walked up their cow to the attic on the third floor to hide her. Someone had reported the cow and the Americans could not find a cow in camp. Frustrated, the soldiers made a deal, you show us where the hell you hid the cow and we will let you keep it. Showing the cow on the third floor and the stairs the cow walked on made everyone laugh about the cow story for days.

Our family was also into the black market. We raised a pig from a piglet to one so large she could not get up. We also had geese and I remember how they were force fed just like the two brothers with oatmeal in Oberlenningen. You inserted food into their beak and then with your hand you held the neck of the goose and massaged the lump of food down the neck. It was a wonder how the geese put up with that kind of treatment. What would the organization Peta say to that kind of feeding. I also had a rabbit that was my responsibility. He was a fat one and had big ears. I will always remember picking grass for him on the hillside above our camp. The sad day came when it was decided that the rabbit was big enough to eat. This was a nutty thing to do. They give me a pet and then kill him. They got some serial killer to kill my rabbit because dad could not do it. The rabbit screamed for help and I heard him, yet did nothing. This rabbit event bothers me to this day.

The Americans wanted us kids to be happy so they decided to have a chocolate bar drop from a large plane. Each bar was attached to a small paper parachute and dropped out of the plane. This happened on the hillside and forest. There were maybe a hundred kids and the plane came over and instead of bombs dropped the candy bars. The kids were running around picking up candy, climbing trees to get the candy, we had the best time, thank you American air force for being so nice. Being nice was part of being American. So what has happened today? We send in bombs and drones and no more candy drops. Also at this time we realized that the Americans were a clean people and decided to get us cleaned up. They decided to give us toiletry goods but we were not used to toothpaste and powders. So the kids took the tooth paste tubes and opened them up and put them on high cement, brick walls, fences and when someone would walk by they would stomp on the tube and shoot out a gob of tooth paste at some passerby.

We had no toys so we went looking for German weapons and bullets in the fields and woods. The bigger older kids got the bigger explosives and guns, they played with them and lost fingers, hands, eyes and sometimes lives. This was not that common but it happened. The big trick was to smuggle the stuff past the guards at the gates. The little guys, like myself were happy with some German bayonets we smuggled into camp and lots of bullets. The bullets we put to good use. You stick the tip of the bullet into an old fashion keyhole and push down, the tip comes off and you pour the powder in a can. The more powder you collect the bigger the flash you get when you light it, great fun. What would the safety minded government agencies tell us about such toys. We must have gotten a little carried away with our toys because the camp organized a collection campaign of all discarded weapons and threw them into a dammed up river, right above the dam. We were disappointed to see belts of machinegun bullets thrown in the river. Think of the powder wasted. The little guys thought maybe some bigger kid could dive down and pull up a few belts of bullets. Nothing like that happened. We were forced to go further and deeper in the woods to find gun powder. So not be too disappointed we invented another unsafe toy. We took an old fashioned key that was open like a little tube and filled it with match head scrapings and packed it in with a close fitting nail. A string was attached to the nail head and the other end to the key head. You held the contraption by the top of the loop, about a foot and a half. You now swung the contraption into a cement wall with the nail head hitting the wall. The pressure inside the key caused the match scrapings to explode. The nail went flying out of the key and you had a big bang. We never figured how dangerous this contraption was. It was a miracle no one got hurt because everyone had them.

I think at this time I went for a little while to a German school while our camp was setting up

Lithuanian classes. To explain the difference between the horrors of our school system today in America and the German class I had to attend at that time I would just present my first impression of the German class. We walked into class dressed, like for Sunday school, Nazi uniforms were not worn any longer. We went to our assigned seats, we had back packs and carried our own little green chalk board. We sat staring at the front, the teacher walked in and we stood up and said "Guten Morgen". We sat down and looked at the teacher waiting for instructions what to do. There was no thought of looking to the sides or talking or goofing off. We learned and we learned, discipline dominated our school day. Today I talked to one of my teacher friends who substituted for one week at a black school in Chicago and I was shocked and afraid for the future of our nation. She had the third grade for one week and could not bring them under control, filthy language, noise, talking, more talking and more noise with no control to get anything done. It was like a zoo or bedlam. It is a small wonder that the Russians and Americans grabbed up the German scientists on their race to space.

Some of my school friends.

We are being marched to school

In Schwabisch Gmund my friends and I were always happy. No one was shooting or bombing us, no one was dragging us off to Siberia. Good food or bad food, no matter what, we were happy. It sure is great to just be a kid. I am on the far right.

Schwabisch Gmund, one of our formal functions. Lithuanian girls are the prettiest in the world.

Schwabisch Gmund-my parents standing in front of our school house

Lithuanians love to dance, I am on the far right.

Our own schools in camp opened up and I was there for my grammar school, second and third grade. I remember my outbursts in class about certain groups of people, the communists, and the teachers comments on how someone so young would be filled with so much hate. Well I had grown up listening how we were signed up to go to Siberia and how my little aunts and grandma were deported to Siberia. I had to blame someone.

We played a game with the chalk drawing on the street where you had to throw a stone on one square and then jump over it in other squares and back. We had a small creek close by and I decided to build traps in the water to catch fish. I put in little wire nets in the creek and only caught tiny fish which always got away from me. The winters were nice, my dad and I would always go sledding on the hills next to the camp. We also went skating with no skates, our street shoes, on the frozen river. The Ice had no snow and you could see the bottom in some places as you moved on the ice with just your shoes, simple pleasures but so much fun. One day below the dam, we were on the ice, and my friend Rimas R. fell through the ice and I helped him out. We were walking home when he turned around and started back to the hole in the ice. "What are you doing", I said. He explained he lost one of his gloves in the hole. Goes to show how important things were for us. I stopped him and we went home.

Schwabisch Gmund, our family, Jonas, brother of Ksaveras, mother, father, me with my boat toy, Ksavers, Ona, grandpa. This is the dam where the machine gun bullets were tossed in to prevent us kids from having fun with the gunpowder

Schwabisch Gmund-my parents and me with my boat by the dam where my friend Rimas fell through the ice

My First Communion picture in Schwabisch Gmund in
May 24, 1949

Our First Communion Dinner, I am on the far right.

Our First Communion Grand March in front of the old
German army barracks building. P.S. If you look at the
roof you see the knock outs with the windows, that is
where I crawled on my butt from one window to the other
to get into our locked room. This was a very crazy stunt.

This is my friend and neighbor from Kaunas, Lithuania, Vida. It was a fantastic coincidence that after fleeing Lithuania in 1944, suffering bombings and deprivations, we should meet again for our First Communion celebration in 1949.

Just the boys from our First Communion. Life is truly strange, two of the group died from alcohol, one became a criminal. I am in the last row on the left.

Our First Communion group picture with parents.

From this town I have a lot of memories. First movie I ever came across was the Jungle Book story of Mowgly. It was such a big thing to have a movie in town for kids. We played simple games, I only had one toy, it was a small metal ship you wound up and the prop would push it on the water. There is a picture of me and the ship. I figure maybe this is why I like boating so much. We also went crabbing in the river and also tried to catch bigger fish, trout, under rocks with our hands. There was very little success with the fish, but some of the older kids did catch some, bears do it all the time.

Our next big thing was the first communion, cute picture of all of us. I even had three friends I saw in Chicago. We were such cute little boys and when we grew up my very good friend Richard S. ended up an alcoholic, my friend John P. ended up a convicted burglar, and my friend Arunas R., also an alcoholic ended up living in Colorado, life is weird.

I also went to school in the camp. I believe, second and third grade because I got placed in fourth when I got to Chicago. I knew nothing of politics except what I heard from relatives. I developed opinions about Jews because they were being blamed for communism and were collaborating with the Russian invaders in 1940-1941. The first story I heard was of Grandpa going to town during the German occupation and seeing a group of Jewish acquaintances held in some cage in the town square. They called him by name and the Lithuanian partisans allowed grandpa to get near them. The partisans were local men and all knew grandpa. The Jews asked grandpa to talk to the partisans to release them. It seems the partisans were rounding up all the local Jews and holding them for the Nazi's. Grandpa knew that during the Russian occupation a lot of Jews were happy to see the communist invaders and collaborated with them. It seems that the Lithuanians that were shipped to Siberia were listed by local Jews as enemies of the Soviets. Grandma and the two aunts, Jane and Elizabeth were deported to Siberia. The partisans who had lost relatives in prisons and had family members deported were in no mood to make deals. So Grandpa just talked to the caged Jews but could not get them freed. A world turned upside down were innocent and guilty are lumped together and justice is blind, and God is absent. So grandpa left and so did the Jews . . . with the Germans.

Today we can analyze the type of people that the soviets wanted to deport. They were larger farmers, military people, policemen, teachers, good Catholics, all leaders in a community. Get rid of them and no one will argue about the new Soviet paradise. The deportation happened at the end of one year occupation by the Russians.

So then I guess it is understandable that after each occupation the persecuted took revenge on the collaborators.

Let us get back to our happy time in Gemund. We lived in the attic, in a room partitioned off from the rest of the attic. We had a lock on the door and that could have been a tragedy for me. One day I came back with a bayonet I found in the woods and snuck it by the guards at the gate. I had to hide it in our room but no one was home and the door was locked. The roof had popped out windows on the whole length of the roof and there was a window in our room. You can guess what I did, I crawled out on my butt on the slanted roof through one of the windows and the shimmied on my butt to our private window to get into our locked room, insane, yes, and on a four story building.

My next insane incident was crawling on the back of the army truck transporting metal beds in high stacks. I was sitting inside on the tailgate hitching a ride when the load of rusty old metal beds shifted toward the back and compressed my legs against the tailgate and the rest of me leaning backward over the tailgate with the beds pressing on me. I do not know how I got out of that one with minimum bruises.

Our protest sign in Schwabisch Gmund against the Russian
and Lithuanian communists coming to our DP camp to
persuade us to go back to their communist hell

Another protest sign in different languages.

I do not know what my parents did that I seemed to have so much free time. We were all over the place, my friends and I. There must be a God that looked after us. I remember one incident that seemed as nothing then, but today is a horror story. I was walking in the basement of the barracks and a middle aged woman stopped me and said she does not know how to light the gas stove in the large room and gave me matches and asked me if I could go into the room and light the stove. I was so happy to help this woman that it did not dawn on me that she was afraid to light the match in the room for fear of an explosion. Later, much later, I realized what an evil bitch this woman must have been to risk the life of a young child.

The times in Gemund also had a lot of humor, between the Americans trying to find our pigs and geese to the visits from the Russian soldiers who came to persuade us to go back to liberated Lithuania. Russian soldiers accompanied by Lithuanian communist troops would hold huge meetings in big halls and pass out posters, leaflets, all praising the communist paradise. The speeches were all the same, we love you, come back, everything is great. Then the real noise started when people started screaming about the dead, the tortured, and the deported. Everyone started throwing everything they could find or had brought with them, at these lying bastards. Pure bedlam ensued, fun was had by all as shit flew from every corner and the screaming was heard all over the camp. The Americans could not understand such resistance to talks of paradise on earth. The Russians with the traitor Lithuanians ran for their lives with the American escorts. If not for the American soldiers our people would have hung all of the visitors. The whole camp area was covered with the ripped up propaganda papers. This happened several times and I think that the commies figured out that no one will ever go back to their paradise and stopped coming. The Americans were also perplexed by our behavior because they were still calling the bastard Stalin, Uncle Joe.

I also got into sex at this time. Not really, just joking, I had a little girlfriend Audrey K. She liked me and we played together. One day by the creek in a very private place we were sitting on the grass and decided to find out what it was that made us different. We decided to show each other our very private things, you know what I mean. We saw them and so what. We did not do anything, we never did this again. What we did not know is that now we were sinners. I did not confess this at my first communion because I did not know it was a sin to look at a little girl's thing. The priest never mentioned THAT type of sin when we were getting the education for first communion.

Finally Crossing The Ocean.
[Fall of 1949]

ALL OF US DP's wanted to leave Germany, it was an occupied country under military rule. The German industry was destroyed and people were still cleaning up from the bombing debris. We were living in military holding camps and all of us were trying to emigrate to other countries. America was the first choice, then Canada, Australia.

I believe these countries had a quota system for different groups of people. America had a sponsorship system were someone here would put up some collateral in America and guarantee your support here. My grandfather's brother Karolis Pozela made some papers but they did not work for some reason. Eventually my father's cousin, Mrs.Uksas, wife of Tony Uksas got the papers right and we ended up in Hamburg waiting for das Boot, [Boat-a joke]. Tony Uksas had married dad's cousin, a Krumplyte, who had gotten herself pregnant in the coal fields and had an illegitimate daughter, Ona, who was adopted by

Tony Uksas and eventually married a Ben Mazeika and was one of the nicest, most loving relatives. Tony also had a son by Krumplyte, Tony Jr. who married a nice lady Bernice, but they never had children.

So in a nut shell we had to have sponsorship papers, and many, many health tests to come to America. Mental health was a big concern then . . . so how come there are so many really stupid people in America today. Where the tests flawed or is it inbreeding or pollution causing our problems today. My poor dad had to be searched for the SS tattoos and questioned about the jobs he held in Lithuania. No Nazi collaborators of any kind where allowed into America. The only Nazi's allowed in were the rocket scientists.

The health tests were a pain, constant blood samples, constant vaccines and always pissing in the little jars to pass the urine test. Many older women must have had sugar problems. I always went with my mother for the tests, I do not know why. My mother tried to help the ladies with the sugar problems so she made me give my urine samples to all these women. I must have pissed a gallon for some of these tests that my mother gave away. I wonder how many women got to America because of my talent to have great urine. I should have demanded money for each sample, I would have been a rich little kid.

We finally boarded the big ship, a military transport. I do not remember clearly the name but I think it was like a General Blachford or something like that. On the ship I was placed in the huge men's sleeping area. The bunks were in rows of twos and going up maybe five or six sets of twos. I was placed in the bottom set so I would not fall out from a higher elevation. Dad was given a bunk some where higher. The bunk next to me was a few inches away and the bunk on top was some inches above my face. We had a blanket and a pillow. Every thing was great, I was on my way to America.

Grandpa Juozas Pozela on ship bound for America

The ship set sail or started the engines and we were on our way to the promised land.

The motions of the waves caused our first problems. People started vomiting all over the place. The floors were of metal plate and so the vomit kind of oozed back and forth with the wave action. It was not that bad in the men's sleeping areas. Many good men jumped in to clean up the messes and people learned to get to the bathrooms after the initial experiences. The worse part was at night when someone in the upper bunk could not get up fast enough and vomited between the two bunks. Vomit dripped down on all the men in the lower bunks and then on my bunk, and so the smell was not pleasant. I got used to it and it was not that bad, I was going to America and what is a little bit of vomit.

My dad got a job in the kitchen because he spoke English. He was always coming back with something to eat. Mostly some fruit or some juices, I remember pineapple mostly. I was never sea sick except one time going upstairs to see the ocean in one of the corridors I ran up to the water fountain, leaned over it to get a drink and saw it was full of vomit. The ocean, on the days we were allowed to go on deck, was unbelievable. The swells, hundreds of feet wide, rolling and rolling around us and this is the first time I think I saw flying fish.

Things were great for my dad and me. My mother on the other hand was having problems. The women's quarters were situated in the front part of the ship and there was more wave action felt there. The women had many little children with them and were not as quick to clean up the vomit and diapers. The smell in their sleeping quarters was so terrible that it is impossible to describe. If Dante had visited the sleeping quarters and smelled the smells and heard the moaning of the women and the screaming of the children he would have made that into a circle of hell. My father and I found my mother and saw that she did not look good and was very unhappy. My father being a nice guy offered some fruit and juice to my mom. I think she came close to hitting him that time. She had not eaten or had anything to drink because she could not hold anything down. We wished her well and ran out of there.

The next few visits to mother showed us that she was doing worse and worse. She would not eat and her eyes started bulging out. I do not know if dad or mother or someone noticed she was dying and by some miracle she ended up in the hospital room with an intravenous feeding tube. She was out of that hell hole and recovered right away.

The one other memorable event on the ship was my seeing a burial at sea. An older lady died and was wrapped in a white sheet. The service was held on deck and then, plunk, she is dropped into the ocean. This was mighty scary for a little boy.

Finally we got to New York and disembarked, I do not remember anything about leaving the ship. Maybe my dad carried me and I was sleeping or I blocking that part out for some reason.

New York At Night, and America

THAT IS HOW I saw that great city for the first time. What a sight, thousands of lights, glaring, blinking, street lights changing color, cars honking. To my small brain this was overpowering, way too much stimulation. I believe we were going to the railroad station to go to Chicago and meet our relatives.

America was so good and kind to let us come to its shores, and then they even gave my father ten dollars to buy food and drinks on the train. I do not remember much on the train ride except the dinning car and the black waiters.

Chicago At Night-We Arrived-New Home At Last.

Again at night, we arrived in Chicago at Union Station. Thousands of people all moving, all in a hurry, and the blinking lights and signs and noise is overwhelming. I am only nine years old and not ready for this fast immersion into the fast life.

We look all over for our relatives, and finally, they find us, and we hug and kiss for a long time. Uncle Tony, Anna Mazeika, her husband Ben, my mom's sister Ona. We have our suitcases and head out to find the parked car. I think we drove to Uncle Tony's house and settled in the second floor apartment of his three flat that he used as collateral to write up our papers. I think the uncle moved upstairs with his son and we took over the second floor. The apartment was completely furnished and had all the clothes of my dead aunt. She was a very large woman and my mother wanted nothing to do with a dead person's clothes. The apartment was well furnished and had a large player piano with hundreds of music rolls of Lithuanian music.

We were finally in America. 3520 S. Emerald in Chicago. Anna Mazeika and Ben lived on 3215 S. Green Street. This was very close to St. George church and parish. St. George was the oldest Lithuanian church in Chicago. We explored the area slowly and got acquainted with the neighborhood. There was a buzz around us as we were introduced to more relatives and the friends of our relatives. We had many relatives, distant ones, of my dad. It seemed they all owned a tavern on some corner in Bridgeport. Uncle Tony's son, Tony also owned a tavern on 35 th. and Lithuanica. My dad would go there and take me there sometimes. While he stayed there Uncle Tony jr. would give me a handful of nickels to play in the slot machines on one wall to keep me busy. Maybe that is why today I like gambling and enjoy playing slots.

The three flat we lived in was truly our family center. On the first floor Ona and first husband, Ksaveras Kaunas and grandpa, Juozas Pozela lived. On the second floor we lived, my mom Felicija and dad, Leopoldas. The third floor Uncle Tony Uksas and his son Tony and wife Bernice. We were introduced to friends of our relatives and were relatively happy to be out of the D.P. gestalt. On Sundays we went to mass at St. George church and I was shown the parish school that I would soon register in. I do not remember our first Christmas in America, but I know I must have gotten some presents.

The life in Bridgeport was strange to me because I was always with only adults. I had no friends in the first weeks in Bridgeport. I was like a small prop in a stage play. Adults were very nice to me but I had no one to play with and even if there were some kids outside, I could not speak a word of English. Things changed fast, as they always do. Parents were able to get jobs through friends and relatives taking them to where they worked. I could never figure out how my father got a job at the great Morison Hotel in downtown Chicago. There he was a college graduate, one of the youngest directors in the great cooperative Lietukis in Lithuania, now got a job as bell boy at Morison Hotel. Gone was the chauffeur with the Mercedes, gone were the maid and nanny and my poor dad was now a bell boy thanking the American business men for coin tips he got for bringing their suitcases. I believe it was a miracle of sorts that I never heard him complain about life. He always smiled and seemed happy. Today, I think, was he crazy? I could not have survived that fall in status. You climb so high from a dirt floor, where you were born, to a top position and salary, a thousand litai per month, and then you lug suitcases for nickels and dimes and speak broken English. What a great man he was, what great inner strength he possessed, and I never knew that as I was growing up. Today as I realize the fall of status my mother and father had to endure I appreciate all their efforts to live and survive much more. I do not believe today I could survive, if I ended up in Brazil as a bell boy, and continue living on beggars' wages and some cruzeiro or centavo tips while I prattle in broken Portuguese.

I believe my dad got that job through Anna Mazeikas husband Ben, or Benny, who worked in some hotel as an elevator operator and was the nicest man, always happy, always smiling. Ben probably took dad to some hotel contacts and got him that job.

Life had dealt Anna and Ben a sad blow when they had a baby girl that died of pneumonia. Visitors to their home in winter came in and hugged and kissed the baby while they were covered with snow and their clothes were frozen cold. The baby got chilled, and got sick, and died. Anna was very religious and wrote it off as God's plan. This helped her cope with the loss.

Anna worked at Hart, Schafner and Marks, I believe, and was stitching button holes in vests. It was hard work because it was piece work. Guess what that was, you got paid on what you produced. What would happen to our economy if all the lazy workers were paid on what they produced? Anyway my mother got a job as a seamstress. She lied her way in and when she sat down by a huge sewing machine she did not even now how to turn it on. She explained that she had never worked with such modern machines. So she was taught on the machine and started sewing furniture upholstery material. My mother worked with many foreign women so there was always somebody there to translate if she had problems.

I could not be allowed to stay home and recuperate from the war, so I was taken to register at the catholic grammar school, St George. No one straightened out my age problem and because I spoke no English and my scholastic records were screwed up, so I was registered in fourth grade.

Things were mighty scary at first, surrounded by the big nuns with their weird flowing robes, a lot of priests all over, and everyone speaking English. Things are not always as you first perceive them and I found out that all the nuns spoke Lithuanian, and I believe all the priests did also. The American classmates, were not all American, I believe a third of the kids were Lithuanian D.P.s. I was assigned a boy that spoke English and Lithuanian sit next to me and translate.

School was great, I soon learned how to walk to school by myself and carry my lunch. I did my lessons, went to church with the class and the nuns.

The nuns had the little clickers that told us when to kneel, stand or sit. I prayed, went to communion and wanted to levitate in church to impress my friends. I believed in all the Jesus stories and said the Stations of the Cross.

My most traumatic religious experience was going to confession one day and telling the priest I missed a Sunday Mass because my parents did not go that Sunday. The priest said that it was my duty to go and because of that he would not give me absolution until the next day. Here I was about ten years old and damned to hell for all eternity, boiled in tar or oil, my skin blistered, eyes popping out of my head if I died before I could get absolution the next day. My companions for eternity, Hitler and Stalin suffering next to me, what would they say to me. I oozed home along the walls of stores on Halsted Street, staying away from cars. I am sure I did not sleep well because I knew people died in sleep. That was known as the happy death you would earn if you had said some novenas on certain days. I did manage not to die and was glad it was not in the plans of God to cast me to hell for eternity. I got the absolution, the next day, but I was sure my plans to levitate in church were gone because of my Mortal sin.

Aside from my religious trauma things were going very well. I made friends very fast and learned English faster. I made friends at that time in Saint George School that became my life long friends. I lived very close to a boy I met in school, Romas Burneikis, we met walking home and became very good friends. I also met the Rackauskai twins, Saul and Ray. It seems that their mother, a widow, and my mother were friends in Lithuania. From school I met the Perzinskai brothers, George and Henry. Some of the kids I hung around more were Henry Stankevicius and Faustas Antanaitis.

Saul and Ray Rackauskas with their mother. Our friendship started in fourth grade and continues to this day. This is when they were in high school.

A lot of the stores on Halsted between thirty second and thirty fifth were owned by Lithuanians.

There was a small store on the east side on about thirty third that had candy and many little toys and a used comic book pile on the counter. The comics were my great love at that time. They sold the used ones for a nickel. I loved the Lone Ranger, I wanted to be like him, always fighting for justice. I was fascinated by Indians and their adventures. I think I learned a lot of English from comic books. Our comic books had moral values presented to the kids. The bad guys always lost, even the Beagle Boys in the Donald Duck comics always came to a bad end. Looking today at how our kids are entertained and comparing it to the past we have to be shocked. At that time the educational gurus tried to enact a decency code and ban bad comics. Today we are giving the kids the most violent games, comics, and movies that have degenerated into murder mayhem and illicit sex. Today queers are on a lot of shows portrayed as great people and entertainers. They want to marry and adopt kids. What happened to my world? When did it die? Who destroyed our standards, our morals, and who perverted our principles of justice, honesty and fairness? Everything is ok today. We attack countries for no reason. Our government spies on us, our crooked banks are bailed out by us, criminals are roaming our streets, illegals cross our borders at will, we have, today, lost the immunity a nation has to have to survive.

I learned a lot in those few years in Bridgeport. I learned that some of the Americans did not like DPs and so some of the American boys would chase us but we always outran them. Once Romaldas and I got caught by the little devils and I tried to bribe my way out by offering them a pencil I had. For many years afterwards I could not live that down because Romaldas always laughed so hard when he remembered that. I wished I had stuck that pencil in the little American asshole's eye. I think we had some coins and I bribed our way out of that trap. The fact that we were picked on by the American boys came through to my mom also. One day we were going to the Jew owned fruit store on Halsted Street when we had horse shit thrown at us. We asked "Why you do this?". they told as that since I was Romalda's friend and he had become a real pain for them, they were getting me as his good friend. I was very nearsighted and could not see the bad American boys from far away, so I bought a tiny telescope for ten cents at the comic book store, I mentioned before. Now I was able to identify the enemy from a distance. I also took the telescope to class because I sat in the back and I used it to see the blackboard. The nun spotted me and asked me what I was doing, told her I was looking at what she wrote on the board. Well she made me come up to the front row and asked me if I could see the board now. I could not see what she wrote even from the front row. I was told I needed glasses. This was a real shock to me because glasses at that time were perceived as sort of wimpish. I had a double problem now with a name like Valentinas or Valentine I now had to also get glasses. In school, especially on Valentine's Day I got a lot of teasing. How many times I heard, Valentine be my Valentine. Anyway the nun, I do not remember her name, gave me a note to my mother about having my eyes checked out. The nuns all had odd names like Pancreatia, Mary Agatha, Sister Mary Joseph, I always wondered what idiot picked these odd names for them.

The biggest shock about the glasses came to my mother when she realized that her child, the perfect child was imperfect, nearsighted. She rushed me to the eye doctor where I was tested for glasses. The doctor announced that it was a miracle. My ears perked up I was still praying to levitate. The miracle he said was that I never got hit by a car. Imagine a boy with no absolution going home and he can not see cars. How close can one live to the edge?

My poor mother now tried another way to make her son be great. I was signed up for piano lessons with a nice woman teacher, a wife of doctor Gudauskas I believe. Every week I went for lessons and came home and practiced on the player piano. I learned to play Twinkle, Twinkle, Little Star and The Campbels Are Marching. The lessons were going on for some months and then my mom was told by my music teacher that I will never be a piano player. Thank God for that honest woman. I did not like playing the piano, I had no talent playing the piano and therefore I should not have been given lessons to play it.

Life was great, I had my own bedroom, great food, lots of chocolate, bubble gum with Bring Them Back Alive jungle cards. I collected comic books and in the evenings with Romaldas we would go up on people's front porches and watch their TV through their front windows. The people were good neighbors and did not mind, we were never chased off. The TVs were small and some were round. The shows were either some dippy singing or tap dancing or some old cowboy movie. Everything was black and white, life was simple, we were happy.

Ona and Ksaveras bought a TV and so I would go downstairs through the back porch to the first floor, to visit and watch TV. There were no lights on the back porch and so, at night, one had to feel his way down the stairs to Ona's back door. One night as I was feeling my way down the back stairs with my hands in front of me I walked into a giant wet fur swinging in front of me. I grabbed onto it and thought that this huge, fur thing grabbed me, I screamed at the top of my lungs and just about peed in my pants. Ona opened her back door and saw me hanging on to her wet fur coat, that she had cleaned up and hung on a rope outside her door.

Again things were back to normal and now I started to go see movies with Aunt Anna Mazeika. It was weird, why she always wanted me to go with her to the local theater, Ramova. She never cared when the movie started, or what was playing. We would just come in at any time and when that part of the movie came up again that we started on, we would leave. It is strange today that this never bothered me. Anna loved the Shirley Temple movies the best. Later I figured out why she always took me to the movies.

The Ramova Theater gave out free dishes on certain days to ticket buyers. You got big dishes, little dishes, cups, all the same design, gold and purple colors, Anna was collecting a whole set.

At the Chicago beach with Ksaveras standing, uncle Benny, my mother, sitting, me, aunt Ona, Uncle Tony Uksas, my father, aunt Anna Mazeika.

The school was easy and I did not push myself to excel. I played with my friends and kind of did not much. I visited Romaldas and in his back yard he had a huge pet rabbit and a cat. We would let both out at the same time and the rabbit would try to mount the cat. We thought that was strange and funny as the cat always got away.

On Sundays we all went to mass at St George and then to a dinner at Anna and Ben.

It was always a typical Sunday. The mass ended and as we were leaving the church, a young priest always waited for the people outside, on the stairs, a Father Prunskis. Anna always gave him five dollars, as many other people did the same. My parents never gave him any money. It was a strange ritual to observe every Sunday after the dinner we all piled into the Pontiac that Uncle Uksas owned and went to St Casimer Lithuanian Catholic Cemetary. This cemetery was bought and paid for by Lithuanian people and because they were so religious and ignorant they assigned it to the archdiocese of Chicago. Years later our Lithuanian cemetery had the word Lithuanian removed from the name. How stupid are we and how unfair the church is to do that. Anyway, at the cemetery we visited the graves of relatives, watered the flowers, pulled some weeds and then drove to Kean Avenue in Willow Springs where there were maybe three or four Lithuanian picnic groves. There were so many Lithuanian religious clubs, singles clubs, trade associations, parish clubs, and all of them threw picnics. There was always great food, lots of drinks, and a lot of dancing. My dad was a very good dancer and all the older ladies and widows did a lot of dancing with him. People got together and sang. There was a special candy game always on a table, you pulled out a bunch of candy with your hand and guessed, odd or even, if you guessed right you won the candy. If you did not guess right you had to pay so much for each candy. Great game because you always got the candy and I never had to pay, some relative always paid.

Here were also the forest preserves where we walked around or someone took the kids horseback riding. We all had a great time and then toward evening uncle Tony took us home. Tony junior and his wife Bernice never went with us. I think they believed themselves more sophisticated, then the picnic types.

When we were out of school we hung around the houses we lived. There were no computers, no TV, so we climbed on things, explored our garages and nosed around looking at everything. When more of us got together we played some games, we also went to a boys club a few blocks away to see what was going on. The club was strangely called Valentine's Boys Club and was located on Emerald Street. I never did much there, but I remember watching a woodworking section which was interesting. We also had Halloween parties there, I liked to dress like an Indian. We always went and collected a lot of candy. We never worried about poison, needles, razors in our candy. It was a great time to live, an innocent age. The school work was progressing along and we also had Lithuanian lessons at St. George, thought by a strange, nice man, Apolinaras Bagdonas. He was never able to control the class and we abused him terribly. He would make us stand in a corner and we did not mind that. The interesting thing about Apolinaras was that he was a teacher for a long time and was always appearing at all the Lithuanian functions. He was almost immortal, I think, I went to his wake in 2009 in December. Can anyone believe he was my teacher in 1950-51-52 and died only in 2009. I was truly happy to be at his wake to say goodbye to a nice, weird, teacher that I felt close too. He was actually only ninety seven when he died.

We had fun at the school and the nuns organized a Christmas show for the parishioners and parents. They wanted everyone to see how talented we little ones were.

I could not act out my favorite part as an Indian but was given a part with other boys of tap dancing Uncle Sams. We had top hats and flag type shirts and tap danced in a line waiving our hats. Soon we were asked to perform all over the world . . . we were not.

The next fun thing that happened at the parish was that the priests invited a carnival to set up in the school yard. This was entertainment and a fund raiser for the parish. The carnival had rides and games of every kind. I always went with parents or relatives and went on all the rides and played all the games to win prizes. When they thought I had enough fun or they ran out of money I went off by myself to have fun. This was the time I became a con man, or little boy con. I approached little old Lithuanian ladies and spoke to them in Lithuanian, telling them how I wanted to play some games and win some prizes but had no money. My favorite game was the ping pong ball toss into little glass jars with goldfish in them. The ladies that had not met little DP boys that talked perfect Lithuanian always said how strange that the little boy can speak such perfect Lithuanian. I almost always got nickels, dimes, quarters to keep gambling to win those goldfish. Carnivals were fun and profitable.

At home we always played some games like running, hiding, climbing. We always managed to survive. One time we tied a rope between two fences and jumped over it. Romaldas was more athletic and cleared the rope. I got my foot caught on it and slammed my face into cement. My front teeth got pushed back. We learned that you had to leave the rope loose when you want to jump over it.

One time I remember we got Uncle Tony pissed. Romaldas and I jumped from the back porch into the small yard on wet grass and completely tore up the lawn.

Things were not all fun and games. I helped around the house and always went to the little store next door to get milk or bread. I also went shopping with my mom and I remember going to the shoe stores on Halsted to buy shoes. The shoe store I think was a Red Goose brand store and had an x-ray machine where you could see the bones of your toes to see if the shoe fit well. This was always interesting and the kids loved seeing their toes x-rayed. Fun was had by all and the shoes fit well. X-rays were not harmful then.

Young Karolis Pozela, brother of my grandfather Juozas, beginning his wrestling career in Russia to become a world champion. You can Google up information about him using the name Carl Pojello.

We also during this time visited grandfather's brother Karolis Pozela and his wife Olga who was a Russian Jew, ex-balerina. Karolis at that time had a wrestling, boxing, gymnasium on thirty second and

Karolis Pozela, famous picture showing how unbelievably strong he was

Halsted. It was in a large commercial type building called Milda. Karolis at this time was a promoter of wrestling and only wrestled rarely as the masked marvel on TV. Years back Karolis had been a world champion wrestler. He wrestled in Russia, China, Mongolia, Japan, Europe and the U.S. Karolis always welcomed Romaldas and me and we were just getting interested in becoming some kind of athletes there when Karolis closed the place down for some reason. He died of cancer in 1954. Karolis and Olga lived on the gold coast in Lincoln Park in a high rise apartment. We would go there for some parties were we met some of their famous wrestler friends. The building had a door man and elevators, this impressed me very much. The guests impressed me more, one of them was Maurice Tillet, the French Angel, he had a hydrocephalic head and looked like a monster. He was the nicest guy and entertained me by showing how he would take a handful of walnuts and crush them in his hand. At these parties mom and Ona would talk broken Russian to Olga and surprisingly I picked a little bit up of Russian and impressed my aunt, Jane, in Lithuania years later.

Aunt Olga, Jewish-Russian ballerina, wife of Karolis Pozela the wrestler.

My uncle Karolis Pozela and the French Angel.

We also visited Karolis to go to the north avenue beach. Karolis had money, he would have had more if Olga had not had a gambling habit at card playing. The card playing as I heard was busted up by the police at one time. Olga however was very good to us and loved me very much. She had no children so she wanted to help me become Americanized. She started by getting me a more modern haircut. I liked to wear my hair long but here in America the boys had crew cuts, flat tops and looked like clones. In those days looking like everyone else was a good thing. Individualism was not regarded favorably. After I was getting to look more American Olga took me to see Alice In Wonderland.

Uncle Karolis, as I called him, drove a huge Packard black car, if I sat in the back there was so much room that you could run around there. We visited some places with Karolis but he was busy with the wrestling promotions and we ended watching some wrestling shows featuring the Angel. The audiences booed the Angel and cheered when he got beat up. One time he was being punched and knocked around and seemingly got mad so he picked up his abuser and smashed him on his knee and threw him down with disdain, this was nice to see. One other wrestler-boxer Karolis tried to teach was a Lithuania by the name Vinca.

My uncle Karolis Pozela and wife Olga when he was dying of cancer in the 50's. Today, sixty five years later people are still dying of cancer and our government allocates a few billion dollars per year for research but wastes trillions on needless wars.

The other interesting fact about the gymnasium was that in the same building, Milda, there was the communist Lithuanian newspaper published. It was called Vilnis, and was run by the first wave Lithuanian communists, it had the office in a store front on the street level. I never did anything to them, but Romaldas would run in there and yell, curse at them and push things off their desks and run out into the street and we had to run like crazy because the people came running and yelling after us.

These attacks on the communist paper increased as our friends in Bridgeport found out about the paper. We hated the communist where ever they were and Americans were also fighting them in Korea at this time.

My language skills improved, I read a lot of comics and began to look deeper into word spelling. One of my problems was the Meigs airport on the lake. I could not understand how America permitted Russian Migs to land by our lake while we fought the Migs in Korea. The other word was Sun-Times which I thought was called Some-Times. Was this a regular paper or what? The last word was Faker and I thought it was the bad F word.

One other traumatic thing happened which might have been the thing that shaped my life in some odd ways. I was hit by a panel truck on Halsted and Thirty-Fifth Street. We were playing, and I ran out between cars and got bumped in the head. I was happy that the driver had good reflexes and did not run over me. Peopled rushed up to help me but I got up and seemed ok. After telling everyone I was ok I walked home and went into a closet and shut the door holding my bumped head. I sat in the dark closet for a long time and I remember I wanted to become like the Lone Ranger. I would emerge from the closet, wear a mask and fight crime. I wanted to become a super hero. My headache went away and I left the closet but abandoned the idea of wearing a mask. School and parents would not understand a masked little boy. Yet all my life I am driven to fight for justice and truth. I hated the invasion of Tibet by China, I hate the lies religions preach, I hate the warmongering of our own government, could all this be caused by a bump on the head?

As all things change and end or begin, our stay in Bridgeport came to an end because we bought a six flat and a restaurant on Cullerton Street and Morgan. The neighborhood was a working class ethnic type, called 18 th. Street neighborhood. The parish we joined was a Lithuanian Parish called Providence Of God. I attended the sixth, seventh, and eight grade.

I left my friends with some sadness, the Lithuanian DP kids now ruled Bridgeport. Our boys were the most lethal in Bridgeport now. We no longer were DPs. We were the worst ones there. Names like Piggy, Zeke where known all over Bridgeport as some real tough kids.

Eighteenth Street

TWO YEARS IN America and we are able to buy a six flat with an operating restaurant. Is this a great country or what? It is an old, old frame house, with a bowed out wall. It is sided with asbestos siding but no one knew or cared about that problem. The address is 982 W. Cullerton, it is on the corner of Cullerton and Morgan. The house is a two story building with four apartments upstairs and the restaurant with some rooms, and a big apartment in the back part on the first floor. The first floor is heated with radiators and a coal burner in the basement. The second floor four apartments are heated by individual oil stoves. The second floor apartments have no bathrooms or bathtubs or showers. There are in the corridor two little toilets that have only toilet bowls. To shower the people on the second floor have to go through a very dark long walkway in the basement that has many rooms along the sides that are not finished or even have floors to find the shower stall. Dim lights and a cold, long walk, with no bulbs along the way, so a lot of times we washed up in the kitchen sink.

As a kid I never knew that it was a disadvantage not to have a bathroom in the apartment or that as a kid I would have to carry a five gallon oil can two blocks and then drag it home trough the snow and constantly fill the oil stove. I did not know that we were poor. That is a great advantage in character building. Maybe now I understand why the house in 1952 only cost $11,000.00. We all combined our savings, mom and dad, Ona and Ksaveras and grandpa Juozas.

It is surprising that today I do not remember the name of our restaurant. It was a simple neighborhood restaurant. We had on the counter those plastic towers displaying slices of pies that were always drying out. The dishes and cups had a circular band design and were extremely thick so that they never broke even if you dropped them.

We had the regular clientele every day, factory workers going to work or going home or lunch, stopped by. The neighborhood costumers were mostly a lot of single men who always ate out, they were mostly retired. We had a cook we inherited from the old owner and we had a menu that was very simple. We also catered big factory dinners or luncheons and had twenty or forty people sit down at long tables. We served them limited choices of several different foods, this was a huge effort on mom, Ona, grandpa and myself. I constantly ran from the kitchen to the tables bringing out the food, clearing of the dirty dishes and pouring coffee. I spoke almost perfect English with no accent, I was almost a perfect waiter until I dropped the biggest Jell-o mold in front of everybody during one of the catered affairs. Grandpa at this time was over sixty five and was not a very good dish washer. He believed if you got them wet, they were clean.

Life went on, I drank more Cokes at the restaurant and got used to the weird taste. I enrolled in sixth grade in Providence Of God parochial school and made new friends but definitely kept in touch with Romaldas Burneikis and the Rackauskas brothers Saul and Ray.

We had to ask the people in the second floor, two bedroom apt. to move out and in the meantime I slept in the back room of the restaurant with the rats. Yes, the big rats would start walking around soon after dark. They were on top of the cabinets and you could hear them on the floor. They never bothered me or bit me. I think people make too much of a big thing about rats. At that time I was a little scared of them but then I just covered my head with a blanket and went to sleep. I now had glasses and could see them if I put on the light or the street light through the window cast enough light and I could make out their large grey shapes.

The rats were not good for the restaurant business so grandpa and I decided to kill them. We got large rat traps but the rats were so big that the traps only worked a little bit. The rats just vanished with the whole trap. The city also put out poison in the alley ways and put up signs not to play with the poison. Grandpa also got some poison and spread it around. There where times when there were some rats that died in the passages in the basement and you stepped on them. The dead rats felt like rubber balls under your shoe and you recoiled. The bottom line was that these methods did not get rid of a lot of these rats. Grandpa and I decided on plan B to fight the rats. Grandpa tied a large meat fork used in the restaurant kitchen to a broom handle and made a spear out of it. I loved my grandpa, he was brave and clever and the rats were in trouble now.

We finally cornered a huge rat in the pantry and I moved the stuff off of the floor while grandpa stood by with the spear. When the last box was moved the rat was cornered, but he was a brave rat, he stood on his hind legs and faced grandpa with bared teeth. Grandpa jabbed him in the lower, front chest and skewered the rat like a shishkebab. The poor rat did not die right away and so we had to take him to the alley and work him off the fork into the garbage can. Grandpa was always organized and so he took apart the spear and wiped of the rat blood, made the fork wet and put it back with the rest of the kitchen utensils.

We continued to have problems and fun with the rats for a long time. As we got older we began to hunt them in the basement. It was great entertainment for all my friends and myself. The basement foundations consisted of slabs of layered rocks and the rats had dug tunnels and came out through different openings to travel all over the basement and house. We would in the evening, when they seemed more active, put salami slices in some of the openings and sit on a bar stool with a twenty two caliber rifle and a flashlight aimed at the opening. Sure enough in a short time you could hear the movement and then see parts of the rat in the openings. Bang, and the single shot trusty rifle killed the rat. We used twenty two caliber bird shot bullets. These were twenty two size crimped on the end bullets and filled with pinhead size shot. They were lethal on the rats and our prey did not suffer at all. We were never into torture of any critters.

We of course had a contest of who shot the most rats. I won because I lived there and hunted more times. My friend Justin Rutka had the claim of shooting the biggest rat I had ever seen. We had to bring in more tools than a coat hanger to pull it out from the hole in the rocky wall.

We threw away most of the rats but we did have people that we did not like, so we tied the dead rats with a rope and a coat hanger and threw it over the phone lines or electric wires in front of their houses. The interesting story about this is that the victims of our prank could not remove the dead rats but had to call the city to get a ladder type truck to get the rats removed. So for days they had to look at the dead rotting rats in front of their houses until the city came to remove them. We were very clever, yes?

The basement of this two story wooden house stretched from Cullerton Street to the alley, all the way under the house. It was a very mysterious and magical place for us to play in. It was only partially finished. Under the restaurant there were cement floors. This is where the shower and the heating unit were located. The coal burner only heated the first floor with the radiators. The coal was dumped through a window into a small room and then in the winter either dad, Ksaveras or grandpa would load with coal, a large metal container in front of the boiler and through an enclosed large pipe a corkscrew like contraption would turn all day pushing the coal into the burner, this was ingenuous I thought.

The rest of the basement had dirt floors, small rooms and were unfinished. Some of the rooms had three to four foot mounds of dirt that were never dug out to make a full basement. These rooms stretched from one side to the other under the house. We crawled around, dug fortifications, buried simple treasures, explored, and enjoyed every square inch of this grand playground, a magical basement. As we explored we found that under the restaurant and under the front sidewalk was a secret room behind double walls and secret doors. We went in to look for gangster guns and treasures into our new discovery but found only some old furniture, a lot of crock pots, dishes and men's clothes. Stripped shirts that I believe were from the twenties. The secrecy and the hidden entrances with double walls tell us today that it was some kind of business during the prohibition.

We enjoyed this great playground and set up a shooting gallery for our twenty two single shot rifle that we had. One of my careless friends shot through the tavern floor a few times and the owners talked to my dad about shooting going on in the basement. I forgot to mention that we had sold our restaurant and it was now rented out as a tavern. My poor dad was so ignorant of what we were doing that he said "Boys just playing." It all ended well and we kept on shooting, but never through the tavern floor.

There was easy access to the basement and cats, rats, and thieves were in and out. One day some thieves hid several brand new Brigs and Sratton gas engines. We re-hid them in another part of the basement and the thieves never complained.

Our playground was our basement some of the time. Sometimes we were spooked out of the basement when people who took showers complained that they heard moaning and snoring and grunting. This went on for about a week and we were concerned about these reports. Finally dad, Ksaveras and grandpa armed themselves with hammers and axes and went to confront and seek out the scarry noise. Flashlights jumping from room to room seeking out the dirt piles and in the dirt pile next to the shower and heating unit the men found a bum sleeping and snoring behind the dirt. The bum was asked to leave and the problem was solved for all of us. There was no ghost, goblin or animal and we took our territory back, so much for the greatest basement in the world which provided us with unbelievable entertainment.

I also do not want to forget the attic which was huge and spanned the entire length of the house. The center and most of the floor of the attic had boards but the edges all around the perimeter of the house in the attic had access between the walls. So you had the outside wall, the studs, no insulation and the inside wall of wood lathe and plaster. If something fell between the studs it was lost forever. A cat in the attic, hunting rats, fell in between the studs in my bedroom wall facing the alley. Every night as the cat was trying to get out from the eight foot hole between the studs it clawed at the walls and woke me up. I was petrified with fear because I was sure it was the wild cats in the alley trying to claw their way up the outside wall and kill me. Night after night the poor beast screamed and clawed on the walls. I told my parents that cats are crawling up the walls on the outside to get me but they believed I had a great imagination. The poor beast died and the noise stopped. I figured this out a few years later while I was exploring the attic.

At about the time we were using the basement and attic as playgrounds another boy, my age, moved into the house in one of the apartments. Vyto Stanaitis came from Springfield, Illinois. His father got a job in Chicago rented one of the apartments and then Vyto, his mom and two sisters Dana and Virginia moved in. The girls were little and we ignored them completely. Vyto was a fascinating guy. He was into comic books and drawing comic book characters. Vyto favored Mighty Mouse, this was a superman like mouse that beat the heck out of evil cats. Vyto not having a camera or a lot of paper decided to produce an animated cartoon, his invention was a long paper strip of cut up paper bags. The sections were taped together and had Mighty Mouse drawings every dozen inches or so. Having the paper strip rolled up and then passing it through a shoebox with a window cut in it to be rolled up on the other side of the box allowed us to see the pictures as they moved through the opening of the shoebox. Great fun was had by all. Vyto and I collected comic books and I stored mine in bushel baskets. We knew how to have fun without much. What made us like that?

CHARACTER SHAPING ON EIGHTEEN STREET.

When I moved to the blue collar neighborhood called 18 th. Street I went to 6, 7, 8 grades of grammar school at Providence of God Parish School and went for two years to De La Salle Christian Brothers High School on 35 th. and Wabash. So, in my most formative years of growing up I lived in a poor neighborhood without any community support to make me feel loved, belonging, appreciated, or whatever the liberal morons today preach that the community or government should provide to make kids grow up wanting education, success, and become good citizens. Hello . . . we had as Lithuanian DP's, the one most important element for kids . . . we had a high, educated class of parents, that were our role models for achievement. Even when the parents worked at low paying jobs, night and day, even when we were growing up in the streets, there was in each of us, ingrained an understanding of what is expected of us. We knew in some mysterious way what our cultured, educated parents expected from us. Knowing this expectation set limits on our pranks, games, vandalism. We were guided by some invisible rules to finish school, go to college, and be human beings. The invisible rules were our understanding of the parent's expectations. This was our greatest gift from our parents, when they had no money, careers, or anything to give us.

Today the sociologists, psychologists, load us up with bullshit of why our society is failing in producing great, motivated kids. The answers are so simple, kids fail and turn to drugs, gangs, and real crime because they have shit for parents. Their parents have nothing to give these failed kids because the parents and grandparents come from a line of losers. Uneducated, unmotivated, without any role models, generation after generation produce the same set of losers.

Why were we blessed with these exceptional parents? Why were our parents so great? The answer is very simple. Our Lithuanian DP parents, who came here in about 1950 were a part of the highest class of people that existed in Lithuania during WW 2. Our parents were listed by the communist swine as people that owned property, were educated, and could not be re-educated to love communism. So the educated, successful achievers were deemed by the garbage of society, the communists, as enemies of the state and should be killed or deported to Siberia. That is why about 60,000 of the best left Lithuania to escape death and deportation. Not all managed to escape and so other great role models that were erased from our gene pool were the 30,000 partisan fighters that fought an unwinnable fight for ten years and died. Thousands of remaining great role models were deported to Siberia because they did not fit the communist image of the new man in their stupid world, a lot of them died in Siberia. Some came back from Siberia, broken, sick and not allowed to get a place to live or get jobs. They somehow survived in Lithuania, they were helped by relatives and good people that managed to fit in the communist system and survive the red plague. These returning survivors managed against all the adversity to produce a new generation of great, educated class of the Lithuanians that today have created a nation that is part of NATO and the European Union. Our survival, our achievements in the United States and in Lithuania is proof that a great gene pool and great parents are what is needed to build a great society.

Justin Rutka, my very good friend on eighteenth street.

God, have I digressed from my autobiography or what? Anyway that was my way of introducing our psychological mind set on 18 Th. Street, as we were forming into human beings.

My friends came from similar backgrounds so we kind of fit together well. My best friend on 18 Th. St. was John Rutka. He lived on 19 Th. St. He was one grade ahead of me and had a chubby brother Justin, who was, one grade in back of me. John had an older sister Daiva, who was a bit older and had nothing to do with us. John also had a younger sister Tootsie (Anele), she was a lot younger and did not exist for us.

My other friend was Augie Rimkus. I knew him from the Germany DP camp. He had older parents because Augie a had a much older brother who was a painter, artist, in Paris. Augie also had a retarded brother who was left in Germany because retarded people were not allowed to come to the US. So I ask you . . . what the hell happened between then and now that our country today is filled with retards, criminals and diseased people. The answer is very simple, all anyone has to do today is walk across our border. There are no more tests to take like we had to do to come to America. We have lost our immunity to protect America and our gene pool and we persist in destroying ourselves by political correctness shoved down our throat by our controlled mass media.

Vyto Krisciunas, a close friend on eighteenth street.

My other friend was Vito Krisciunas. He lived on Racine Street and had some older brothers I never knew and a baby sister I barely remember, Ausra.

So in a nut shell there were usually in our group five of us, the real buds, Rutkai brothers, Augie, Vito, and me.

My other friends who lived further away were the Rackauskai twins, Saul and Ray, Romaldas Burneikis from Bridgeport, and Charlie Mikulskis who lived on the east side of Halsted and did not hang out with us.

It was strange when you think today that at that time all my friends were Lithuanian. We had become

Americanized, we spoke perfect English, yet we had only Lithuanian friends. We knew American kids and talked and played with them but we never developed friendships with them. It was some kind of ethnic mentality that was not understood, visible or questioned. No one picked on us anymore or called us DP, we were like everyone else.

PROVIDENCE OF GOD CHURCH AND SCHOOL.

Church and school were operated by the Lithuanian Order Of Sisters Of Saint Casimer. Our parents called them Kazimerietes. The sisters were all of Lithuanian descent and spoke Lithuanian with an old fashioned dialect. Some of the sisters, I felt, had a resentment of sorts against the Lithuanian DP's. Maybe it was just me, being very sensitive, that I picked that up from some of their comments.

The sisters all wore the long black robes with the white round bib and the helmet like black head cover. It was hard to tell their age. The sisters had weird names, like sister John., sister Peter-Mary, sister Vincencija, and on and on. They were our teachers and religious guides. The school was next to the church and so we were often marched to church and then back to school.

On certain days we went to confession or went to say the Stations of the Cross. Religion was a dominant aspect of our upbringing. The sisters used the clicker signal to tell us when to kneel, sit, or stand. We prayed and prayed for our souls and for everything else. I think at this time I gave up my desire to levitate in church and concentrated on the suffering of Jesus for our sins. We said novenas to reduce the amount of days we would have to suffer in purgatory. We also said novenas to have a happy death. I never questioned, at that time, how it was possible to pray for a happy death.

We also prayed for the conversion of Russia to the Virgin Mary, and it worked. During class we prayed every half hour with parts of the rosary. Someone in class would ring a little bell, and a short session of prayers were led by different individuals. I hated to lead the prayers when it was my turn, I was shy.

The homework was never much so it never interfered with our street adventures in the afternoon. The sisters graded us on different subjects and also on religion, behavior, with letter grades. G was for good, VG was for very good, E was for excellent and U was for unsatisfactory. Days we missed were also marked and I was truly notorious for missing many days. My mother was always concerned about my wellbeing and I capitalized on that with every bit of fever or sore throat I could conjure up in the morning. One day one of the nuns remarked that I seemed to always be sick and I retorted that perhaps it was the climate in the US that made me sick. The sister then said maybe I should go back to where I came from. I answered that if I could I would go back. The sister then made a weird comment about me that I did not know how to take. She said "Still waters run deep". What in the hell does that mean? I was shy, yes, I was quiet, yes, I never was outspoken in the class or a class clown or trouble maker. What does a statement like that imply? I guess I will never know.

During the three years at Providence of God we also worked hard to support the school and religious activities. The sisters asked us to sell raffle tickets and we were given quotas and rewards if we accomplished the tasks. The New World Catholic paper subscription drives also pushed us to become pests to our relatives and neghbors. We did all that and enjoyed the time off we got for doing that.

At this time polio was still making kids sick and we were aware of the dangers waiting for us on beaches, pools and crowded places. Also at some point in the grammar school the polio vaccine was discovered and we got series of shots.

Here I was a little kid and had to worry about ending up for all eternity in hell, burning in hot tar, if I made some mistake and commited a mortal sin, I could also possibly get polio and end up in an iron lung or I could get blown up by atomic bombs by evil Russia. To me my World War Two experiance seemed more appealing than my new life in America. The atom bomb scare was always there, because at given warning bells in school we were rushed into the windowless corridors and sat on the floor covering our heads. Was I traumatized by all this, no. I did however develop a strange doodling or drawing style on the edges of my notebooks. I kept drawing planes shooting other planes or people on the ground. I had the planes that were propeler driven fire two machineguns from the wings. I still do not think there was anything wrong with me, even today, I think I am normal, no matter what I doodled.

EIGHTEEN STREET GAMES.

We played crazy games in crazy places. We played "It" on railroad boxcars. There was a small railroad yard with a few empty boxcars left unattended every evening and so we tried to catch one another climbing up to the top of the boxcar and then getting off at another end. Crawling through open doors to get to the other side was also a good way not to get tagged. We were all over the boxcars and had great fun. No one ever fell off or hurt himself. Now I could see how today this would have been considered completely unacceptable and dangerous. This game developed our muscles, balance and competitive spirit, compare that to fat out of shape kids playing computer games today where they explode, and kill competitive soldiers on a little screen. What is better for the body and mind?

We also would tape twenty two caliber bullets on tracks but never stuck around to see them shoot off.

Our vandalism was not extensive. We liked shooting out street lights with BB guns. This was a fun sport and no one got hurt. It was very competitive because we kept score for everyone. John Rutka and I were tied but John cheated and shot some in the mornings when he did his paper route. The bulbs where large, like grapefruit, and thin glass. When you hit them at the right angle the bb would put a hole in the bulb and roll around inside. The bulb would then smoke through the little hole and get very bright and then go out. This honed our future hunting and shooting skills. The most fun was to shoot out a bulb in front of some houses where people were sitting on their front steps or porches. They were always surprised as the bulb either exploded or smoked, got bright and went out. We liked to entertain ourselves and neighbors. Few times the police spotted us but we dissapeared into gangways and alleys. No one ever got cought shooting out lights.

We rarely damaged private property with bb guns. We also rarely damaged private cars or stole anything. We did break of a car antenna now and then when we decided to make zip guns. The antenna had a perfect size to fit a twenty two caliber bullet and we fastened that to a particular type cap pistol with a hammer that was filed. The whole contraption was taped and rubber banded. After shooting one shot the zip gun would fall apart and we had to tape and rubber band it again. I wonder how many kids would know how to make a zip gun today?

We never tortured any animals or shot cats or dogs. Today we hear of ugly stories of kids tying cans to a cat's tail and then dousing the cat with gas and letting it go in front of people after lighting it. We were truly good kids with just a touch of badness.

We did shoot pigeons, but always for a good reason. Justin Rutka and I decided to learn taxidermy, so our first lesson told us to skin a pigeon. We took the rifle walked over to the railroud yard and shot a pigeon. Imagine doing this today. You would have been classified as a gang banger instead of nice kids trying to learn taxidermy. We took the poor pigeon to the attic of my house and skinned it according to the manual. We did not know what to do with the small skinned body so we decided to throw it out from the attic window into the alley. As we looked around we saw one of the bag ladies comming up the alley with a little cart looking for good garbage. We decided not to hit her in the head with it but to throw it in front of her and surprise her. As she saw this chicken like thing fall in front of her, she was completely confused. She could not figure out where it flew in from or was it a midget chicken apparition. Justin and I laughed at her confused reaction for the longest time.

Lesson number two called for skinning a cat and boiling the flesh off the bones in a large pot. I imagined my mother finding a boiling cat skeleton on her stove, in a pot, and decided with Justin that we did not want to be taxidermists.

We did shoot some more pigeons but it was also for a reason. There was across Morgan street a Bohemian butcher shop and the owners wife would come out on Morgan Street and feed pigeons. We would crawl out on our roof and peek over the peak and see the little old lady feeding about a dozen pigeons all around her. We had a pallet rifle that had a good amount of power and we were able to kill the pigeons around her. They flopped around and fell over while she fed them. She never heared the rifle or saw us. We laughed so hard we almost fell of the roof. The little old lady was so confused about the flopping pigeons.

Where else can young boys can have so much fun. You created, and invented fun things to do. There were no limits on our inventivness except our counsciences. We pitched penies on cracks in sidewalks. We flipped gumball cards against walls to see whose landeed closest to the wall, that person won. I remember laying on my bed and shooting flies off the ceiling with a bb gun. Where could you do that in a suburban home? You say what about the ceiling? It was very old, the ceiling, and it was that wood lathe with globs of plaster squeezed into and evened out. Age made that ceiling cracked and lumpy, gobs of it always fell down and we would do a so, so, patch job on it. A few bb dents never showed up too much.

When it rained we played cards inside. The game was called hearts and when you lost all the other players got to hit your knuckles with the deck of cards, it hurt and your knuckles bled. When we got bored of hitting each other with the cards we thought up of things the loser should be forced to do. My favorite punishment for the loser was to have him wear huge bat like cardboard wings on the arms, fastened with ropes and hide in the alley behind garbage drums at night. When an unsuspecting lady or girl would cross the alley the loser would leap out from behind the garbage drum and run past the woman flapping the wings and yelping bat like sounds. The rest of us watched this great event and thought it was the cleverest trick ever. We never asked the women what their impression of this was. We saw them jump to the side and scream as they were startled, but I am sure they mostly thought it was just very weird. Some probably went home and said they saw a vampire in the alley. At that time there were movies of vampires, warewolves, and mummies, we saw them and were fascinated by them. We kind of were spooked by the dark, maybe, just maybe there was something about all those stories that could grab us in the dark.

One time I was walking with John Rutka at night when I felt something run up in back of me and put pressure on my shoulders, like hands, and I felt the hot breath, hot saliva on the back of my neck. I sreamed so loud and jumped so high in front of John that I believe I scared him more than I got scared. It was a huge, very thick furred large dog that wanted to be friends. I scared the dog, and he ran off, John was shaken and I almost died of a heart attack. For a split second I am sure my mind said, vampire, when I felt the breath and hot saliva. It is ironic, or poetic justice that a perpetrator, me, of so many pranks should experience such a great prank by a dog. Makes one think that God sometimes has fun with us.

We had very little homework so we spent most of the time on the streets. I came home from school, did the dishes in the sink, and always had the cups floating in the soapy water and pretended they were sinking battle ships. All the guys had hobbies that seemed trendy for some periods. We all had tropical fish and loved the guppies with the long colorful tails. We watched the guppy females have live births and tried to catch the babies and put them in separate tanks. We built model ships and planes, we collected comic books. Life was good. We always had fun and never cared about our clothes or realized we were poor and lived in a poor neiborhood. It was great to be so free of serious thoughts, and responsibilities and we also never thought of the future. We lived day by day, pranks and adventures, on and on.

The neighborhood also had some tough older boys that had a dress code, smoked, had duck ass hairdos, the DA. They hung around certain houses or corners. They hardly ever bothered us. They knew us local kids, paperboys, they mostly left us alone. One summer however they came up with a game they played on smaller kids. The summers were hot and in the evenings most of the people sat on their front steps or porches to cool off. The older boys would grab a smaller kid and strip him down and then take all his clothes and put them in the middle of the street. Then when the little guy was released he had to scamper naked into the lit up street to get his clothes. The older people could not believe their eyes seeing a naked kid running around the streets. This was weird and funny for everyone except the little naked guy. None of our group ever suffered that. We knew when and where to avoid the older kids.

The smaller kids paid back the smart asses in their own way. On hot days as we walked by the older boys who wanted to show off their power over the little guys, so they would say," Hey do me a favor run over to the candy store and get me a Coke". The kid entrusted with the job would go to the store and use the dime to put in the Coke machine and take out a bottle, and open it. The Coke machines were horizontal with metal tracks holding the bottles. The coin would release the gates for one bottle. If the owner was not watching, a smart kid could open a locked in bottle with his bottle opener and use a straw he had to suck out part of a Coke. Now the kid would open the bottle on the side of the machine and start going on his delivery. It was so hot on some days, and kids wanted just a little sip of the Coke. The kid sipped off about an inch or two of the coke and now had a problem of delivering a not so full bottle. Not a problem for us clever kids, we just pissed an inch or two into the Coke and the cool guys never knew. I never did that but I wondered how much Coke can be replaced with piss before the cool guys noticed. It would have been worth a lot to do that experiment and imagine telling the Coke company that you could mix Coke and piss fifty-fifty and not taste the differance.

The cool guys with gang jackets did not bother us but we must have had some fear or dislike of them. We shot one of them . . . with a pallet rifle . . . what did you think from the first few words? We were in the attic and had the window open a little bit facing Cullerton street. The cool guy with the leather jacket was strutting east on Cullerton and accross the street, I nailed him in the back and he jumped up like the pigeons that were hit. We ducked down and he never knew what hit him or from where. He probably found the small hole in his gang jacket. We did not do much of that, we mostly did pranks.

There was a Lithuanian guy that had an apartment house and never liked us sitting on his cement stairs.

He had two daughters, one had big tits and the other one had hardly any tits. We had begun to notice girls at this time but had no idea how to be their friend. One day someone got a rubber and we all spit in it and put it over the doorknob of the apartment building. I wonder what the man made of that prank? The next trick we pulled on the poor man was an old trick of filling a paper bag with dog shit and then lighting it and ringing the doorbell. The first thing anyone does when they open the door is try to stamp out the burning fire. This prank always created a lot of laughs among us.

The fun and games continued. It was as if time stood still and all we did was have fun with never a thought of time moving and us growing up. In Providence of God we prayed and learned. The nuns were good teachers, we had discipline and in De La Salle highschool we had the Christian Brothers who were stricter and had the right from someplace to hit us. Maybe that is why with all the imposed discipline we played so hard and broke so many rules.

While in grammar school I got a job walking two younger kids home. They were in second or third grade and were unique in the fact that their heads were shaved and the heads had very bony features. My friends and I called them little bone heads. I never knew their names and got paid fifty cents a week for walking the little bone heads home. I got fired from the job because the mother saw me talking to my friends and the bone heads ran into the street.

Summers seemed long with nothing to do except play. We finally got a book mobile from the library to come once a week on Racine and Nineteenth Street. I became an avid reader and read all the stories of the Indian Chiefs and western heroes. I also read classics by Jules Verne and about King Arthur. We were allowed to take out a lot of books and I remember having a problem getting them home. I believe the interest in books prevented me from getting into more serious troubles.

Our parents also tried to entertain us in the long hot summers. On weekends, on Sundays after mass and a visit to the cemetary we went with Uncle Tony Uksas and Anna and Benny to the Lithuanian picnics on Kean Avenue. A good time was had by all. Our restaurant was run by other owners and my aunt Ona was married for the second time to a new guy, Stanley. He tried to show us a good time also and we went to a drive in movie where my mother almost lost her fingers. In the drive in movies you parked next to a post that had two speakers, so you put one in the car through the window. When you went home you took the speaker out and replaced it on the post. While my mother tried to get the speaker out Stanley hit the gas pedal and smashed my mom's fingers, bent the post, and almost cracked the window. Stanley was not known for his great driving skills. When he was learning how to drive, he drove into a Lithuanian restaurant on Halstead Street and broke a man's leg who was sitting there eating. This was the Auditoria restaurant on about 32 nd.

We also visited grandfather's brother Karolis Pozela, the wrestler, at his gold coast apartment. We sometimes took rides in his big black Packard.

Back on Eighteen Street we had only one theater, the Milo theater was a short walk west on Eighteen Street. We went to the theater, not very often. My mother did not collect those dishes.

We also became proficient in using public transportation. One day the guys took inner tubes and a small pump and we went to one of the public beaches. We had the best time but we paid a big price for that fun in the sun. We learned about sunburn and really suffered with ugly blisters and brown spotty scars. Summers moved slow.

Some of our more peripheral friends, also lithuanian, where getting into some serious troubles. John P. Was leading a little gang of burglars that specialized in robbing houses when the owners were at a funeral of someone from the house. The cops figured out John's method and cought them at one of the houses. Another tough guy was John K., who stole from stores and had a friend nick named Crazy Horse. They showed us all the little things they stole from the dime stores and told us how easy it was to steal from the big stupid stores. We were impressed but soon found out they all got cought and that took out any ideas we might have had.

Crazy Horse was really crazy. We knew him as a guy that would do anything on a dare. If you asked him to shoot street lights, on main streets, that were huge and had thick glass covers with a twenty two rifle, he would do it. He was amazing and we were impressed in a weird sort of way. Was he crazy was in back of our minds? He told us he could steal a pallet pistol from a small store-tavern in Summit. John Rutka, Crazy Horse and I would take the bus to the end on Archer avenue and then walk into the Village of Summit. Crazy Horse and us would walk up to the counter and ask the clerk to show us some pallet pistols. The pistols were in boxes and had a lot of wrapper paper in the boxes plus instruction booklets, and other packing material. As soon as we had the counter loaded with three boxes Crazy Horse asked to see a fourth pistol, another model. The clerk went to get the fourth and that is when Crazy Horse put a pistol in his jaket and when the clek came back we thanked him and said we had to go. Out the door we ran like crazy to a deep gully with railroad tracks and so we ran and walked out of Summit in the bushes, grass and railroad tunnels and bridges. We eventually made it to the start of the Archer bus line and took the bus home. Crazy Horse was not happy just going home, so we opened the bus windows and he was shooting at store windows. It was a real adventure.

A prank that was truly funny was the "crackle ball trick". These pea size, round explosives, Would explode when slammed into cement. The explosion was like a small half inch firecracker. It was fun shooting them out of small slingshots we made out of coat hangers. We would walk down alleys at night and spot a lit up window in the houses by the alley and see a dinning room lit up with a center light and the family sitting around the table eating supper. Three of us would stand outside the window and fire the crackle balls at the ceilings. The explosions would cause total cofusion. People probably thought it was their electrical wires shorting out. We always had a chance to reload and blast them again. We never got cought and simply walked away. Where can you have such fun, not hurt anyone and see the people so scarred and jumping around.

The crackle balls were a lot of fun. Simply putting them down on the sidewalk in front of the store and watching people as they stepped on them and they blew up was also a lot of fun. We also targeted girls as they walked along a brick wall. The explosions on the wall made the girls look around, panic and start running as we laughed ourselves silly. The best crackle ball trick I ever did was when I was an usher at State and Lake Theater in downtown Chicago. Our ushers' changing room was next to the men's room and one day I placed about five crackle balls under a toilet seat, as someone sat down on the toilet seat the crackle balls exploded. The ushers and myself all ran out into the main toilet room and saw a guy stumbling out of a toilet stall with his pants around his ankles and a cloud of smoke following him. We all said what happened and my victim just blurted out that the toilet seat just exploded under his ass. You have to admit this was very funny.

As we got older some of our pranks got a little more vicious. It was interesting that we specialized in pranks and jokes. There was no drug use at that time and we had not started drinking. Perhaps in our senior years we started drinking but until that time it was just fun and games.

I can not leave out our fun with busses or public transportation. In winter time we would have one of our guys wait for a bus to stop on the corner while the rest of us with snowballs waited around the corner. The bus stopped and opened the door and the would be passenger would step aside and the rest of us clobbered the bus driver through the opened door with a dozen snowballs. Sometimes the attack was very succesful and we had a lot of laughs. The bus driver had to be quick in closing the door.

We also for some strange reason resented sight seeing busses. There were some of them on the main streets and people in the bus seemed to look at us as if we were fish in a tank or some animals in a zoo. We always responded by showering the busses with rocks. I am sure people on the tour bus always remembered eighteen street.

We also bought little bottles of stink perfume and just before we got of the bus we would spill the whole bottle on the floor. The stink was of rotten eggs and sulfur and the bus riders never knew what hit them.

Another favorite trick was to have one of our guys on the bus and one of us would run up and with a wad of tape and a large firecracker and glue the mess on the back window of the bus. The firecracker had a burning cigarette spliced across the wick so it took a while for it to explode. The fun part was to have our friend tell us how all the people ran to the front of the bus and were in a panic mode. We believed this was funny. I never knew of the window blowing in and hurting anyone.

We evolved as we grew older and we faced new challenges. The blue collar neiborhood was also changing. Factories were closing and our restaurant business was sold to another owner who also was not very successful and the restaurant was finally rented out to two men who converted it to a tavern. We also as DP kids had at this time our first experience with black people.

LITHUANIAN DP KIDS MEET THE BLACK PEOPLE IN OUR NEIBORHOOD.

Black people moved in next door to 982 W. Cullerton, so what. We did not care, because we had no set opinions of black people. The American kids whispered nigger, nigger, burr head, we said what the hell are you talking about?

Ever slowly we began to learn about the black people and started to develop a belief system and eventualy a racist attitude. Whose fault was it that people developed beliefs and then attitudes, about a group of people. We certainly did not develop our attitudes from pure imagination or pull them out of our innocent Lithuanian butts.

I would like to cite some examples of how our next door neighbors behaved. First they crawled into our basement and wired their three flat to one of our meters. The next month's electric bill was five times the normal amount and my poor dad went to the electric company and in his broken english tried to correct it. Maybe the meter was broken or something he said? After some research we found out our black people neighbors had been stealing our electricity. My dad and Ksaveras did nothing about it, they simply disconnected the wire. I do not know if the bill was paid or not. We should have set a trap for the black electrician with a burried electrified mesh. When he crawled in to rewire he would have died by electricution. Is this the right thing to do?

The blacks had about a million little kids in that one house. They all played along our house screaming their heads off. The gangway in the basement along our house was covered with boards and so we went to the basement and stuck in cherry bombs, large firecrackers, between the boards, and started yelling so the black kids would gather around the boards to see what is going on and we would light the cherry bombs that exploded and scarred the little monsters home.

We would stand sometimes talking in our second story corridor and look into the black neighbors back yard and porch. One day a young girl sixteen-eighteen came out on the back porch. She did not see us by the window so she hicked up her skirt, dropped her underpants and pissed on the porch and stairs. My friend and I were horrified, shocked and did not even bang on the window or open it and scream pig, pig. She just went back in to the house.

The next time we were standing by the window a little boy of seven or eight came out on the back porch with a little girl the same age, they both removed some of their clothes and the little boy tried to rub his little limp penis between the little girls legs. They tried to do what they saw the older blacks doing in front of them. My friend and I were in shock and told all our friends who could not believe what we saw. Now maybe I understood that the only place we saw black people were in circuses in europe.

We still did not call them niggers nor hate them, we simply were surprised at their animal like behavior.

We did pull of some great stunts on them. We somehow got a bow with target arrows and played with that for a while. We would go out in back of the building and shoot up in the air. The arrows came down in the alley or hit the roof and stuck there. One arrow went into the black peoples back porch and stuck into it while a black lady was washing something in a bucket. I calmly walked into their back yard and wiggled my arrow out of their porch and walked out. I said nothing to her and she said nothing to me. It was strange this silence. The arrow could have killed her or hurt her. We stopped shooting in the back of the house then. It was also hard to retrieve the arrows from the roof. If my dad would have found out about our bow games he would have said, "They just playing".

The bow games went to the railroad yard where we shot arrows into the air straight up and then tried to catch them as they came down holding our arms in a circle in front of us. This today I consder our most stupid game kids can play and I place it ahead of our bb gun fights with no goggles that we did later on.

There were no other blacks in the neighborhood so we played some pranks on the next door neighbors. My most memorable one was of us making large airoplanes from heavier stock large sheets and setting the left wing to ressist air so it would turn left in flight. We would tape an m-80, or a cherry bomb, light it and sail it out the attic window. In the late evening the blacks all sat on the front stairs and the plane would turn and fly right at them and explode scarring the shit out of them. This again was great fun and exiting for everyone. We sure knew how to have fun. Can you compare that to any computer game?

We also shot cherry bombs with slingshots. One person would shoot and one person would light. We had a great system to play with cherry bombs. We would also throw a cherry bomb in a garbage can and put the cover back on. When the bomb went off the cover flew about thirty feet into the air.

The big firecrackers are now illegal and the government has decided that it is up to them to protect us.

It is no mystery how prejudice comes about. We had none to start. When we witnessed the garbage type behavior we began to dislike the blacks and tried to live further from them. The politicians constantly preach about prejudice and how we should be politically correct yet they miss the basic root cause of prejudice against blacks. The blacks themselves are the root cause of discrimination and prejudice. Learn to speak correct english, dress properly, behave properly and you yourselves will accomplish what the stupid government tries to shove down our throats. Give the nation positive beliefs and the attitudes of people will change for the better. Simple example is that the blacks showed their true colors during Katrina and the Japanese people showed their true colors during the tsunami catastrophy.

OUR SEXUAL AWAKENING ON EIGHTEEN STREET.

Sometime in the latter years of grammar school we started getting interested in girls. They were persons of interest but we did not figure out what we wanted to do with them. We liked some of them more than others but we had no idea how to approach them or say anything to them.

On the streets we got a hold of some eight pagers depicting cartoon like charecters having sex. We began to understand a little bit about human anatomy. Pornographic magazines were non existant. There were no magazines that showed female models showing pubic hair. So we were limited in our sex education. The nuns and priests only barraged us with the possibility of going to hell if we even put ourselves in some situation where there was the occasion of sin.

This avoidance of sex education, lack of any printed material we could learn from, and the constant threat of everything to do with sex as a great sin produced in us a confused mental condition. The condition was aggrevated by our sexual maturation.

We would have liked an answer as what to do with our boiling hormones.

In the early fifties and mid fifties we were left to our own devices as to how to handle sex. Girls were frightened to death of pregnancy and of commiting sin or of becaming an occasion of sin. We did the best we could to cope with our problem. To say it politely, we handled the problem ourselves, individually.

We did not talk much about this problem or share our experiances with our friends.

Masturbation was discovered by each one of us in different ways and then came the improvement of the different methods. Maybe now some of us started thinking who needs girls. This practice moved with us to highschool and was popular with all the boys. We all pretended that we did not do this. My friend Virgil told me that an old, down to earth Christian brother, in De La Salle, a brother Josephus, told his class that four out of five boys masturbate and the fifth one lies.

The Christian brothers at least acknowledged that boys masturbate and there were romors flying around school that if you have pimples, are shy, blush easy, have bad eye sight you are probably a masturbator. We were told this was a sin and had to tell the priest that we played with ourselves and that in some unimaginable way it hurt Jesus, a God.

It is interesting to try to understand how self abuse is related to sin. Who does it hurt, who does it bother? The simple fact is that self abuse simply happens because we are humans with many animal charecteristics. We noticed at the zoo how the monkeys play with their little dongs. If they have figured this out so can we. Sin or no sin we continued the practice risking all the rumored problems including boiling in tar in hell for all eternity.

I was probably about fourteen when my mother suddenly woke up and became concerned about my penis. My dad went into the Lithuanian army and was then circumcised. Maybe my mother talked to someone or thought I will go into the Lithuanian army, or maybe she considered that we should become Jews, but I was suddenly paraded to her lady friend doctors who groped me and embarrassed the hell out of me.

I had to go to a hospital, get cut, and share a room with a bunch of grown men who had the most fun teasing me and calling me Romeo. The nurse came in to change bandages and took me to the bathroom to take my first piss. I wonder why she held me while I started to piss. The sensation of pissing with your mutilated penis for the first time after the mutilation can only be described as possibly sticking your penis into a fire. I can understand how the poor Jewish kids developing mental problems from being mutilated.

I did not tell my friends about this nor went around showing girls my new improved penis. It was kept very private. Today I think it would be cute to have a before and after pictures of this adventure. So I had my new, improved penis and still no place to stick it.

The head of the penis being released from the enclosure became more sensative to rubbing or riding on the buss and I was plagued by erections on busses, churches, car rides and it was always very wise to carry a sweater or jacket so to cover the stupid bulge in the pants. Praying for the erection to go away never worked. Taking it out on the buss and slapping it was not a good idea. Hiding it was the best method.

The good thing about masturbation for boys is that it prevents wet dreams. Wet dreams are when in your sleep you feel you are having sex and ejaculate huge amounts of semen. This is a real mess and I just wonder how the priests and brothers cope with those kind of releases. However we must remember that masturbation offends God, in some strange way, and is a sin, while a wet dream is just as much fun and is not a sin. So in order to remain free of sin and be in a state of grace, one must hope for a lot of wet dreams to spice up your life.

SUMMER CAMP AT LAKE PAW PAW

My poor parents working at menial jobs were under the impression that I was not having a great time growing up on eighteenth street. What gave them that idea? Nothing but factories around us, houses squeezed together, smog, heat, nothing but concrete around us. There was no air conditioning. First window fan we bought had speed control and we felt as if we had a demi God in our apartment. What a pleasure it was to have that palluted air blown through our apartment. A small slice of paradise we experienced with that first window fan.

With the heat and all the problems poor people have to contend in blue collar, lower class neghborhoods my parents did not realize that I was perfectly happy there. I had friends and we played in the streets. We did not know that another world existed.

My parents saved up some money and sent me to a summer camp on Lake Paw Paw in Michigan. The camp was owned and run by Lithuanian Jesuits. It was right on the lake. Here we learned a little more about religion and Jesuit discipline. I met new friends, played games, sat around fires and was entertained. Food was good, friends were plentiful and we had a great time.

We had free time from organized activities and spent it in the water, hicking around looking for frogs and snakes or reading comic books. Life was good, it always is when you are a kid. In this camp I had my near death experience by drowning. I love boats, and swim a little, but three times in my life I almost died by drowning. Lake Paw Paw could have been the watery grave of a little DP kid. I had my diving goggles on and jumped off the end of the pier without knowing how deep it was at the very end. My googles got flipped off, I could not touch bottom and there were weeds tangling my feet. I did what everyone is told not to do, I panicked, splashed to the surface, and yelled out. Thank God there was an older, very tall boy, by the name of Romas Bublys who jumped in and grabbed me. I caught my breath and was helped out onto the pier. This was a scarry lesson, but a very good one, because I gained a lot of respect for water. Water should be respected by everyone. It is our best friend, and yet, could kill us if we forget its potential. I never met Romas properly nor thanked him properly.

There was a papermill we toured in town with the camp kids and I think then I decided to be a journalist . . . just joking.

The great leader in our camp was Father Burevicius. A very tough Jesuit that scarred the evil out of us and maybe that is why there were no eighteen street pranks played in camp. He was tough, always fair, and got our respect. Another priest was Father Tomasaitis, a handsome young Jesuit that was wery nice and kind.

Someone in camp was stealing comic books. I somehow spotted this kid doing this. His name was Pete D. we called him Pissy Bingo because he wet his bed. I told Pissy Bingo about a bunch of comic books in one room and then I told Father Tomasaitis that Pissy Bingo will try to steal them when we have the evening fire in the field. Father caught Pissy Bingo in the act of stealing comic books. The crime wave by this master criminal stopped. I do not know what they did to Pissy Bingo, but I felt like a great detective hero.

Many years later when I was the executor of my aunt Aurelija Bitautas I ran into Father Tomasaitis who was working with an evil woman Pranckevicius. The two of them exploited senile old people and tried to steal or appropriate the estates. Father Tomasaitis even told my aunt in her demntia clouded state that he was her relative.

It is strange how people evolve over time. From good to bad, from faith to no faith. I guess the only thing for certain is that change is real.

HARD WORK . . . THE PATH TO THE AMERICAN DREAM

Justin and I worked at the Naujienos Lithuanian newspaper on Friday nights, inserting the Saturday literary edition into the regular paper.

While on 18th. Street I worked many different jobs. I liked to have my own money because I always wanted something.

One of my first jobs was inserting the Saturday literature edition into the regular paper at the Naujienas Lithuanian newspaper on Friday night. Naujienas had at that time thousands of subscribers and it took us a long time to do this job. My distant relative Cepas worked as a typesetter there. It paid little but was something to do. It is interesting how fate plays with us and I ended up printing the last issues of Naujienas years later in my printing plant, Questar, in Chicago.

One of my weird jobs was selling magazines door to door on the north side of Chicago. I would take several busses to meet the crew managers on the north side and then they would give us certain streets to work. This was always after school and would go on until dark. We followed a special presentation formula telling the people we will give them free magazines of their choice for free because we want to set up delivery like paper routes in their area. We told them that young boys would be hired to deliver these magazines to them weekly and all they had to pay was fifty cents per week for two years for delivery service. Look was one of the magazines.

So . . . the delivery charge cost the subscriber fifty two dollars in two years, but the magazines were supposedly for free. The crew manager then called on the people and told them the delivery system was being set up, or was planned to be set up, and they would be better off paying the fifty two dollars up front instead of being bothered by some kid every week for fifty cents.

In truth, there was no route being set up, so the people became regular subscribers. We, the salesmen gout paid $7.50 per sale. We averaged two sales per evening, so back in the fifties this was nice money. People at that time were making .75-$1.00 per hour. I was one of the few kids that lasted over a year doing this.

Imagine today having a young boy of 13 or 14 going door to door in the evenings in strange neighborhoods, entering huge apartment buildings with not the slightest fear of any danger. Was this a dream or another planet, this could not be our beloved Chicago. I was never in any danger nor was ever bothered by gangs or bullies. I wonder what changed today to make that kind of a job impossible for a 13-14 year old kid?

My one other job that was similar to the magazine sales job was selling supposedly handicapped produced goods. These were kitchen type items such as pot holders, sponges, ironing board covers and similar items. The salespeople, us kids, would meet the managers in a hotel room where our suitcases of goods were packed with marked prices. This again was worked on the north side of Chicago.

We were instructed in our presentations and driven to certain street corners and had assigned streets. We knocked on doors, and told mostly the lady of the house, we represent the handicapped people who produced our goods. We showed them our samples of cleverly packaged goods with a large label on top saying handicapped goods.

The goods were only packaged by one or two handicapped people to make this con game legal. Our managers would hire some cripple or retard and have him package the goods. The prices were very high and we were paid a third of the selling price. The product sold very well because people wanted to help the handicapped people. It also helped for the salesman to stutter, or twitch to make more sales. This job made everybody happy, we made good money, people assumed they were helping the handicapped, and the managers made good money. This selling method worked so well that I was thinking of doing it myself.

We worked in the evenings and no one ever bothered us. We had a lot of money on us from the sales and there was never a problem.

I was still not sixteen and had to lie to get hired by a distributing company, that was hired, to introduce Mr. Clean product in Chicago. The way this worked was that we reported to certain areas where vans filled with sample cases waited for us. Six or more climbed into the vans and were driven to special Chicago areas and told to go door to door passing out samples from our case of 48 bottles. We also had to leave, I believe a .10 cent coupon for the product.

The people in the van were mostly derelicts, drunks, and bums and me. We got paid minimum wages. We paid Procter and Gamble back with kind of work the salary warranted. The older guys, all, stole the coupons and sold them to the stores for half price. I never did that.

The vans were always there with more samples when we ran out. The women loved the free samples and we often traded more bottles for cookies, milk, or soft drinks. It was a fun job, and when you had to piss you pissed in some hallway because it was illegal to piss outside in public, that was the law.

Procter and Gamble tried to track the coupons but the bums always explained they shoved them under doors. Going home with a van still full of samples was bad for our image. We had good understanding low paid drivers who stopped on bridges and allowed us to throw cases of samples into a river. Every one was happy, the samples were gone.

When I attended De La Salle High School I would go downtown and work as an usher after school. Who had time to do homework? I worked at the State and Lake Theater on weekends, also. It was a fun job. You got dressed up in a nice uniform, with a bow tie and worked many different stations. You swung doors open for people, you seated people, you took tickets, you worked out side wearing a cape and an admiral type hat and told people about available seating. After work you made out with the candy girls. It was an interesting job with so many young people to work with and so many nice costumers.

My first real girlfriend was a candy girl at the State and Lake Theater in downtown Chicago. Her name was Jackie C. and she was a few years older than me. After work we would meet inside the theater, in a fairly empty section and begin our kissing and groping. This was most frustrating because we made our hormones boil and sizzle with no consummation. I am glad this romance ended because the most logical conclusion of this would have changed our lives completely. We were much to young for the consequences.

As ushers we pulled many pranks along the way. I placed the crackle balls under the toilet seats. We would direct drunks to the women's bathroom and listen to the screaming as the drunks came stumbling out. We chased perverts and mashers out of the theater. These guys would change seat next to different women and were easy to spot when you were seating people. They would finally choose a victim and then grope her. The chase would then start and everyone was running after the pervert.

I sometimes took tickets, and when the manager was not around, I would sneak in the shoe shine boys on the street to see movies like Old Yeller. I felt sorry for the little kids who worked hard and could not afford the movie ticket.

I believe working hard, always working, is the only good way to find the American Dream. If you have the right attitude you will always be happy working because you will always feel you are moving forward and closer to the American Dream.

OTHER EVENTS ON EIGHTEEN STREET

Eighteen Street was close to Maxwell Street. Maxwell Street was the ever going flea market in Chicago. Every bargain you imagined was sold there. Used stuff, stolen stuff, new stuff it was all there displayed in kiosks, stores, sidewalks. Most of this operation was owned and run by Jews who pushed their products. We shopped there with parents for cheap new clothes and shoes. The stuff was cheaper because the sellers had no overhead or very little and I am sure the kiosks never paid or collected sales tax. Income tax on most of those businesses was not paid either. Our group of guys went there to look for switch blades, knives, firecrackers, key chains and other nonesense. We enjoyed playing around with the Jews by haggling the prices way down and then when they reached our offer price we would say that now we changed our minds. It was always fun to tease them.

The gypsy women were there pretending to sell more than palm reading. We knew they were all fakes and after you gave them a buck or two they would pretend you would get sex and walked you out through a corridor and as you ended up in the back yard they slammed the door and you were out the money. We played them and some of our guys would pretend they would go for their deals. They would fake an interest and then grab and grope the Gypsy and we would all walk away laughing while the Gypsy yelled after us.

We did have sex on our minds but had no idea how to get any satifaction. One day after the trip to Maxwell Street while we were sitting on some stairs a new acquintance by the name of Irwin showed up. I forgot to mention that in 56-57 several knew kids started hanging with us. Our group got bigger as we grew older. There was Irwin a German-Lithuanian and a Henry Schlefendorf same type. They came to our turf later than we did and had totally different backgrounds, morals, and were very wild. They lacked almost any parental controls or had no role models at all.

Irwin tried to impress us that he was having sex. We were all ears on his great adventure. He told us how he went to Maxwell Street using Halstead Street and that from about Seventeenth Street going north to Fifteenth Street you had to go under the dirtiest railroad bridges. No one ever swept or picked up trash there. It was dark, damp and dreary. There were alcoves there where one could sleep or hide. We walked through there in a group and met bums, hobos and bag ladies. These sub humans stayed there to get out of the rain in the summer. Irwin proudly told us how he managed to persuade the mostly black bag ladies to have sex with him under the bridge for a quarter. All of us almost threw up on visualizing what he told us. This to us was very close to imagining eating shit. Irwin could not believe that we did not all want to run under the bridge with a quarter in our hand.

HENRY SCHLEFENDORF

We loved guns. Vyto on the left, Schlefendorf in middle
and me, with 22 rifles in Lemont are having fun.

This was another older boy that arrived late in
our neighborhood. He was a German-Lithuanian,
probably from the Klaipeda area which was heavily
infested with German colonizers for hundreds of
years. Why you ask a paragraph or two for this
charecter. He was truly outstanding as an individual.
Not by what he accomplished, but very simply for
what he did, or dared to do. Was he crazy, or brave?

Henry was a little older than we were but he
wanted to be our friend. He was a very large fellow
with a lot of curly dark hair and bright lively eyes. He

was not fat. He was stocky and muscular. He spoke english with an accent.

Henry was trained in Germany to be a welder, so he got a job as a welder here and made a lot of money and treated us sometimes. We had no money as we all were in highschool and so were impressed with him. Henry bought a red ford converetable and gave us rides. Henry told us stories about his work. One them was about the fact that he always took jobs no one wanted. These jobs were very dangerous and he presented himself as a brave guy. He told us of working on a very high chimney on 22 nd. St. With another guy. Henry was welding and talking to the man and when he turned his head to see his co-worker, the guy was gone. Henry looked down and saw the guy on the ground. The man died from the fall.

Henry had a knack for getting into trouble. We had begun to go ice skating to a skating rink called Michael Kirby's. The place was filled with young people, a lot of pretty girls. We mostly raced around and bumped into each other and fell over. The rink had rules. You only skated in one direction and the organ music was always slow so as to prevent speeding and rough housing. We at first rented skates and then bought our own figure skates. There were sessions during the evening when it was couples only and we asked girls to skate with us. Things were relatively calm and normal until Henry came with us. Henry had little fear of consequences and with his bad english managed to bump into and insult some local tough guys that he challenged to fight outside after skating. We were not told of this and when the four of us came outside we met a mob of ten or more what we call greasers. We had no intention of getting beat up so I think John Rutka started talking and explaining how Henry does not understand things and sometimes creates problems and that now, he is sorry, and wants no trouble. The greasers were not stupid and probably did not want a big fight with tons of people leaving the rink and being witnesses. They accepted the apology and threatened Henry, who we now shut up and dragged away.

Henry pulled the next stunt with the police. He was naturaly driving like a goof and got pulled over by a cop. He was asked for his drivers license and gave the cop his whole wallet with the license in one of the pockets. This was all ok except for the fact he had Hitler's picture next to the license and the cop was Jewish. This made the cop totally unprofessional and he started screaming at Henry and pushed him. Henry's friend another German told Henry to kick the Jew cop, which Henry did. This caused the cop to write up a bunch of tickets for everything and Henry had to go to court to have the book thrown at him. In court he got yelled at and had the book thrown at him by a Jew judge. Henry was not a quitter and so he hired an expensive lawyer and proved that the Jew cop and Jew judge were prejudicial and had all the tickets and all other transgressions thrown out of court. Henry was our hero because we had thought he was going to go to jail.

Henry did not learn any lessons well. He drove like a wildman and at an intersection hit a car broadside and the impact threw the other driver out the side door. We never wore or had seatbelts at that time. Henry jumped out of the car and ran home, he knew the accident was his fault. He immediately called the police and told them someone had stolen his car. The police contacted him later and said that the thieves wrecked his car and they did not catch them. Henry collected the insurance money and lived happily ever after for a little while.

Henry sometimes because of his big size would tease or push some of the smaller kids around. He did that to me and I immediately told him I had two axes in the car trunk and we should take them out and fight. Henry accused me of being mentally sick and never teased me again. I would never had done this and he could have called my bluff, he did not.

Life went on and the last time I heard of Henry Schlefendorf was when I was in college in Urbana at U of I in 1962. I was listening to the radio in my dorm room when the news came on and said that a young man was killed in a head on crash on Cicero Ave. his name was Henry Schlefendorf. Later I found out that John Rutka and Henry had been drinking at the South Cicero Ave. strip clubs and were driving home when Henry fell asleep, crossed into an opposite lane and hit a T-bird. John later told me he was drunk and slid under the dash but Henry hit the steering wheel and broke his back in several places. John said as he sat up he told Henry to run away with him but Henry just let out a deep breath and died, kind of a fitting end for a truly wild and crazy friend.

SEX AND THE CAR CULTURE

Sex was evil in the 1950's but I kept trying.

I try to have fun at parties in spite of the sexual repression that was imposed on us in the 50's and 60's.

Going back to the mid fifties we enter a world of almost total sexual repression. The laws at that time censured almost everything, imagine, it was against the law to show one pubic hair on a photograph. The religious zealots in America were like the Taliban of Afghanistan today, everything was a sin, the kissing, groping, had to be done in a dark movie theaters or someplace on the farm behind the barn. Everything sexual was evil, abortion was a crime and had to be performed in dark rooms by quacks or criminal doctors. Pity the pregnant girl who had no money, she attempted to do it herself. There were no gays at that time because the word, gay, had not been invented yet. Gays were known as queers, homos, perverts and were treated worse than animals. So this was our America as we entered puberty and our hormones were boiling. We must also understand that all these repressions were done to make God happy. Huh?.

So now comes the car, our salvation from the sexual repression. The huge cars with the huge bench seats were made to order for great sex. Bucket seats were not in style at that time.

We were allowed to drive when we were fifteen and a half, a student permit, and by sixteen we had a regular license and were drag racing. The first thing we did was try to customize the car. Family cars were harder to do, but we tried. First we put mirrors on both front fenders, this made the car look better. The auto stores sold hundreds of stupid items to make your car look cool. Continental kits were added to the back, we also extended the exhoust pipe with a chrome addition. We tried our best to be cool. Gas at that time sold for seventeen cents per gallon, so we did not have much of a problem because I was making seventy five cents per hour working part time as an usher at the State And Lake Theater in downtown Chicago. The dashboards always had a Jesus statue. The mirror had fuzzy dice hanging on it. The steering wheel had a suicide knob attached to it for sharper turns.

So we went on dates using our cars. The safest place to take a girl, to make out, was the drive-in-theater. Here it was dark and you were as private as you can get and no cops walked around rapping on your window and checking you out. The drive-ins had intermissions so we went to get refreshments and it was funny to see most of the cars had steamed up windows, so you knew sin was being committed in some way. I do not want anyone to think that the car and the drive-in-theater made things easy to get some crumbs of sex. We have to remember that the religious freaks, the nut cases, had brainwashed the young people about sex. The girls were told that virginity was the highest ideal and marriage was the only path to having sex. The boys were told to respect the girls and not try to corrupt them. Also for the boys, masturbation was denounced and only involuntary wet dreams in your sleep were allowed. So . . . we can see how this made any kind of love play very difficult. There were rules made up of how far you can go in making out. Mild kissing was allowed but anything beyond that was resisted. The natural progresion to healthy sex became a groping wrestling match and ended in frustration for both combatants. The religious freaks were in the brains of all the young people guiding them to deny their sexuality.

This oppurtunity of the drive-in-theater and at the same time the religious restraints that existed, forced kids to think of ways to overcome this problem. Some boys brought alcohol with them and tried to relax the girls, others resorted to lies, telling the girls they loved them. Some invented the going steady approach. This was giving the girl a ring and it meant that you only went out with her. So, between the alcohol, the lies, we tried to survive and get more groping in a sexually repressed world, but God was happy.

This sexual repression by the religious Taliban extended to the parks, beaches, and forest preserves. You always had the police, theTaliban of that period, looking for sin. How many times you were accosted by these guards of virtue can not be counted. You sat in a car, in a park, it was sunset, and you were simply hugging a girl you liked, when suddenly there was a flashlight shinning through your car window and a stupid cop was rapping on your window. I wonder how stupid the cops must have felt going around looking into cars trying to find sin being committed. This persecution of young people went through highschool and through college. Sex was simply evil and a sin and society must keep the young from having fun and do what nature intended for people to do.

In college in the early sixties girls were locked up at night in their dorms at ten or eleven, the boys could stay out all night. No one came forward and said this was an insane discrimination based on sex. This also gives us today a perspective of the existing power of religion at that time.

The automobile, gave us some freedom from the religious fanatics. The intellectual awakening in the schools, the desire to be free, the younger professors, the writers who fought censorship, the anti-war movement all united the younger generation into a renaissance of a new life. The flower children of the late sixties came into being. Sex, pot, LSD, individualism came up so fast and strong that the religious fanatics could not contain it. The pill for women gave them the freedom of expression for their sexual appetites.

A new age came to America, the age of Aquarius. What a great feeling it was to wake up in a world that was free. The road to freedom is without end, it will always find blockades by people who want to repeal abortion rights, repress gay people, incarcerate, in America, over one million people for drug use at the cost of about $40,000.00 per person, per year. The ruling class will try to restrain people's freedom by creating fears of terrorism, promoting wars, and using the failing power of religion to hang on to their power. Religious chains have kept the populations of the world enslaved for thousands of years. The pulpit was the only speaking forum, and the religious zealots used it to control the populace. Mass communication, individual ability to communicate in different ways have destroyed the power of a few fanatics to simply preach their garbage from the pulpit.

Today the world is different and it shows up everywhere by allowing people to tolerate sexual expression. The religious nut cases, the religious zealot freaks, the taliban of America and their communicating monopoly, the pulpit, now have to compete with the internet. The internet educates people and allows them freedom of expression. I believe the whole rotten religious structures of the whole world will fall apart when the internet spreads in their areas. No one can remain stupid when constantly confronted by new ideas, facts, and general information about the whole world. Truth, reason, will win out against religious fantasies and mankind will be set free.

Alcohol Clouds

I am discovering alcohol.

IN THE LATTER part of high school we started tasting beer and some cheap hard liqueur. The trick was to get the older friends to buy us the alcohol. We had no idea how to enjoy alcohol. We drank till we threw up and fell down drunk. Somehow we saw this process as having fun. Some of my friends, including myself belonged to a great, patriotic Lithuanian fraternity, called Neo-Lithuania. Our motto was, Pro-Patria, meaning for our country Lithuania. We were very patriotic because we had a good understanding of what the Russian animals, the Soviet Asiatic scum, the communists, have done to our indepedent country, Lithuania. The fraternity culture was based on the style of Germanic college student fraternities. We wore student type hats, had ribbons, across our chest, used swords in our traditional gatherings and drank like hell in all of our functions. The tradition also had a gathering just for the guys, called an Alutis, translated it would be A Beer. Here we had swords at the ends of the table, the tables were set in a u shape and at the head or the center of the u sat the master of ceremonies. Order was mantained by banging the swords on the tables. The pledges served us beer, we sang songs, told jokes and drank beer. As we got drunker and order was harder to maintain, so we were now punished by the selected sword handlers, they sat at the ends of the u. The punishment was to take a full glass of beer, put it to your lips and by the count of three gulp down the beer. This process led to more punishments, great laughter and complete drunkedness. All of this mayhem went along with the presence and participation of all the older, grown up members. The only thing we had to do as we were passing out was to make sure we would not emberass our colors, the hat and the ribbon. We had to remove them before we passed out.

Our Neo-Lithuania fraternity is great not only in our motto, "Pro Patria", meaning for our country but it also unites generations of members. College students become "Senijorai" after they pledge. After graduation they become "Filisteriai", and throughout our lives we interact at all the functions.

So, you can not fully blame us for being drunks at most functions. We were introduced to this behavior by our elders.

In our homes, during parties with our parents, hard liqueur was drunk not as a mixed drink, but from shot glasses. Singing, drinking, getting drunk, that was the tradition at home and at all of our functions. Each shot glass you drank was accompanied by a statement "I sveikata" meaning to your health.

One of my memorable fraternity experiances was going as a representative of my fraternity to a Latvian fraternity celebration. Their name was Letonia. I went with an older fraternity member. As we entered the great hall filled with Latvian members they took off our hats and pierced them with swords. This was a surprise to me, we had never skewerd our hats.

The Latvian traditions were a little wilder than ours. They drank the beer but they also drank wine from an old horn. This was bad when you mix wine and beer. We sang songs and got drunker. Now came the surprise, the Latvians started shouting, Olimpus, Olimpus. I had no idea what this was until I saw all the drunk Latvians running around and pushing together in the center of the hall the eight foot long tables, then setting other tables on top and more on top, till I belive there were four sets of tables on top of one another, a pyramid. On top you had two chairs and two Latvians singing and drinking while the pledges kept climbing up to pour more beer for them. Even being somewhat drunk this presented a fearfull picture to me, a bunch of drunk Latvians building a high table pyramid and then scrambling up and down this unstable structure. Everything went ok this time. We continued singing and drinking.

Another memorable event occured at this event, a Latvian student was there that looked exactly like me. We were like identical twins. The body structure, the face, the glasses all were identical. Every one noticed this identical twin phenomenan and I had to listen to all the jokes about whose father crossed the border to father kids. My dad was born in Riga, Latvia so I blamed him. There was a lot of laughter about this strange event.

I regret mostly that I did not get his name or phone number, we could have played so many tricks on everybody.

This ethnic drinking culture followed us to college where we drank, threw up, and drank some more. University of Illinois in Urbana had a lot of beer halls. You ordered fast food and pitchers of beer. After getting drunk we had to walk back to the dorms. I lived in the six pack, Snyder house. My friend Walter and I would walk back together.

Walter was and is a great friend. At that time he had figured out how far I would walk before I threw up. He was right most of the time, it must have been the fresh air, times the distance walked, and sure enough right by Newman Hall I would throw up.

Walking back full of beer we were always forced to piss along the way. This is very normal for beer drinkers. One time we transgressed with our pissing. The urge came on as we were passing a building with an open back yard, a window with a screen and a box under the window, what a set up for a good prank. Without thinking that there could be someone in the dark room we got up on the box and started pissing gallons through the screen into the room. Even today I think how surprised the person would have been to see all that piss on his floor or rug. What a great prank this was.

Walking back was always an adventure. We would sometimes take a bottle of hard liqueur into the beer hall and order only Seven Up, and get stinking drunk while the waitress could not figure out why we are so silly from the Seven Up. One evening being drunk I dropped the bottle on the floor and it broke. I feel this was God's hand in protecting me from what happened on the way home that night. I was and still am a collector of mementos in my life. Things that remind me of events, I collect. So . . . I picked up the neck of the bottle with the jagged edges and put it in my jacket as a souvenier. What a life saver it was. We were heading home again in front of Newman Hall. There were three of us, Walter and a friend of mine Lee. Comming opposite of us were three guys, smaller than we were and we somehow perhaps bumped into each other. I do not remember how it happened, I was drunk. All I remember is that Lee ran accross the street as we passed these three guys and Walter's face was suddenly covered with blood. It seems one of the three assholes hit him in the forehead, and with a ring cut him. All I could see was the blood on my friends face, a lot of blood. Somehow as drunk as we were we went after these three assholes. All I remember was that Walter had one of them in a head lock and was pounding his face. Me, being not a fighter, I took out the jagged glass bottle neck and started slashing at the assholes. I can not tell if I sliced any of them. All I can remeber is them being surprised and jumping back from me. I am sure this bottle neck saved me from getting beat up. The next thing I remember was seeing someones side of a head, close cropped hair and an ear. I remeber hitting with all my might that side of someones head and the head and person dissapeared over some bushes.

Walter was still pounding away and then there was just us standing. Everything in my head was fuzzy and all I remember was going back to the dorms and the bathroom to wash the blood.

Summer camp for our fraternity, Neo-Lithuania. Here we are on a lake, left to right, Saul, Chris, Iggy, and me.

Our summer camp in Cape Cod for our fraternity. Left to right, John, Al, Giedre, Arunas, my girlfriend Terry, Romas, Jone, Baby Huey, Algis.

Making another beer and booze run for our Neo-Lithuania summer camp in the trusty black Simca. John and Casey in the car.

Neo-Lithuania summer camp and me in love again.

Neo-Lithuania summer camp and our Chicago group cabin and me.

A Neo-Lithuania summer camp when we were pledges. We called ourselves, "Fuksu Blokas". Saul is on the left, I am in center and Chris is on right. I think they are holding me up, we also had to wear black hats as pledges.

Neo-Lithuania summer camp always had the traditional flag raising every day with all our colors and everybody present

Walter told me he ran into these three jerks at a football game and they recognized each other. He says they looked like they ran into a truck head on. This little incedent shows how easy it is to get into trouble without meaning to get into it. We could have easely killed or crippled one of the bastards.

Drinking during and after the college years posed many problems. Driving drunk was not considered that serious, so . . . we constantly drove drunk. You know you drove drunk when you could not find where you parked your car in the morning. I always found my glasses behind the toilet bowl. Everyone always drank straight shots. I guesss mixing drinks took away from the time for straight drinking. It always seemed we were in a rush to get drunk. We drank mostly VO, Christian Brothers, Asbach Uralt, and a lot of cheap stuff like Old Crow.

There were also drinking games. The whole gang of guys would go to a nice restaurant and throw dice on the table taking turns. The first person to roll up a pair would order a specific drink, something weird, like a Pink Lady or a Green Grasshopper or a Zombie. The dice would be kept rolling and the next person to roll up a pair would have to pay for the drink. The person to get the last pair would have to drink the concoction. You can imagine people mixing these strong weird drinks and the results, mostly vomiting. The game lasted for a while but some of the unlucky players would be hard to control and the game ended when we were asked to leave. This ending was almost always the same.

One other game we played was interesting. I had found a bar a little further north of our area that sold a small glass of dark beer and a shot of cheap, cheap whiskey for twenty five cents. This was funny because it was so cheap and tasted so bad that we played pinball machines and the winner had to buy the loser the drinks. Nobody wanted to be the loser.

Our Lithuanian fraternity camps for one week, once a year, were the worst drinking binges. At one of the camps, YMCA camp, I think in Ohio, we left a pile of beer cans and bottles that was about four to five feet high in back of our cabin. Someone would always be the biggest drunk on a certain day. The older fraternity guys would stay up and nurse the completely drunk member all night long. I was so drunk on one bottle of blackberry liqueur that I threw away my glasses in a field. My friends crawled on their knees to find them because they knew I was blind without them. My friend Saul was so drunk one evening that we tried to keep him out of our cabin by locking the door. This did not stop Saul, he got a running start and dove in trough a screened window.

It is amazing that with so much alcohol so many of us survived. Some of us did not. Some died in car accidents, some became incurable alcoholics. Some young people had that gene that made them into drunks. The God given gift to most of us was that we were intelligent, had great responsible parents and were lucky not to die in car accidents or drown. The fact that most of us were pressured to get a college education also limited our flight into alcoholism. We were to a large degree responsible.

Union Pier, Michigan beach outing. Friends Richard and Alex.

A great beach outing, young healthy beautiful bodies, sun, water, alcohol, if this was not heaven than what is? My girlfriend is the third from right on the tree trunk.

My own escape from alcoholism was very simple. My liver began to hurt, I got brown spots on my chest, and the whites of my eyes turned yellow. Does anyone need more signs? I went to my family doctor Adomavicius, he looked me over, asked me how much I drank per week, ran some tests and told me to see him in a few days. I sat in the office and waited for the results. Doctor Adomavicius came in with some papers, looked at me and said, Krumpliali, Krumpliali, using a diminitive of my name, you should go and shoot yourself right now and save yourself and your parents a lot of pain. Huh . . . I said? He continued to tell me how badly my liver was damaged and that if I kept drinking at the same rate I would die a horrible death within a few years. I was twenty six years old. The doctor told me my liver was damaged and I was killing myself by the heavy drinking. This was all it took for the happy drunk to stop drinking completely, I swtched to smoking grass. At parties my friends were still falling down drunks and I had to learn how to have fun without drinking, it was traumatic. I stopped drinking and all my simptoms went away. I tried to follow a health diet, lots of salads. I was rather a lone reveler at all the gatherings.

Our alcoholic functions continued, birthdays, New Years, fraternity events, weddings, and dances all ended in drunkedness for most of us, except for me.

Normal weekends we still ended up on 69 th. Street bars. Club Gintaras, The Playhouse, Knights Inn and many others were constantly filled with stumbling, drunk, Lithuanian young people, except I was always sober drinking Seven Up.

When you look back today you have to ask yourself how was this insanity of alcohol permitted to flourish. Where were our educated role models not to see this. How very many of my friends died of this plague. I was lucky in surviving drunk driving and lucky I had no desire to have drinks because of some gene, and I had a great doctor like Doctor Adomavicius scare the hell out of me on the subject of drinking.

Encountering Greaser Punks and Hooligans

OUR LITTLE ESCAPADE of violence in Urbana is just a small sample of the problems boys face growing up from human animals, retards, mongrels, and low life scum. We were never violent or aggressive but always were confronted by low life, low IQ scum, whose only ego boost was to push someone around. Our government today still does not understand the problems poor people face in ghettoes and poor neighborhoods. How dumb must our politicians be not to understand the plight of young people growing up in bad neighborhoods. Growing up there is like walking through minefields every day. So. instead of spending trillions of dollars on needless orchistrated wars, by our well known neo-cons, we should spend a few dollars to save our children from the bad neighborhoods and give them a chance for life without fear or death. Good idea, no? So call the clowns in Washington and tell them what to do.

I have digressed from the two stories of violence I wanted to tell you about. The first story is about THE BATTLE OF PIMP RUN, it is called that because all the pimps ran, that is our group.

It started out on a nice summer Sunday in Marquette Park, in the southside of Chicago. I was walking in the park with two girls, M and Z toward the area where my friends were playing baseball. Perfect day, all nice when suddenly we were followed by some greaser type daigo charecters. They were walking in back of us and making remarks about the girls and calling me a pimp. We finally got to where our friends were playing and the greasers had to break off and leave. Logically this should have been the end but I believe the ten to fourteen of us went to George and Henry's house to arm ourselves and go look for the greasers.

We armed ourselves with bats, pipes, chains, tools, and a zip gun that shot 4-10 shotgun shells. Henry had the pistol. We went back to the park and found the greasers and chased them out of the park. We were celebrating having won the battle with no blood shed. I think Henry had fired a shot to scare the greasers. We were standing around when all of a sudden there were appearing before us a horde of greasers, about thirty of them, big and small. Their total IQ was probably matched by the total of their shoe sizes. The scary part for us was that one of them was the demented hook, who had no hand but a metal steel hook. It was believed he lost his hand while making explosives.

They were afraid to approach us and we did not know what to do. A stalemate of sorts took place. They were afraid of the gun and we had no idea what to do. As a field marshal today I believe if Henry had pulled out the large zip gun and we would have charged them with all of our weapons they would all have run. This however did not happen and some idiot in our group suggested we walk back some twenty yards to a water drinking fountain. This walking away signaled to the greaser horde we were retreating, so they walked toward us. We were intimidated by their numbers and the hook. At this point two of our fighters went off and sat down next to a man fishing in one of the canals close to us. Ahead of us was a stone bridge about ten feet wide. We walked back from the water fountain to the top of the bridge. The greaser retards walked after us and stopped before the bridge. Now there were only about eight of us on the bridge facing these low life animals. I believe Henry had the zip gun out and that kept them from charging us. The hook was right in front of the mass of greasers. Some of us were asking Henry to shoot the hook. I had a baseball bat and stood on the right, close to the edge of the bridge. My plan was to fight a little bit and then jump of the bridge into the canal if we were overrun. The greasers in front had their hands in their pockets as if holding guns. The situation was very tense and lasted a few minutes. After being asked to shoot the hook Henry stated to us that he had no shells left. This statement by Henry broke the impasse and I do not know if we were charged or if we turned and ran but all I know is we ran like the wind through that great park on a nice Sunday afternoon.

We ran through people sitting on blankets, we ran through kids playing, we ran through people lifting weights. It must have been a horrible sight for the people to see a horde of greasers chasing about eight young men. We could hear the greasers yelling to catch at least one of us. I hit the bushes on sixty seventh street like a buzz saw and crossed the street between speeding cars and into an apartment complex entryway where I rang all the door bells. Some kind soul buzzed us in, I do not remember who I was with. We sat for many minutes catching our breath and shaking off our fear.

I do believe that the reason we all escaped was that the older greasers had been heavy smokers and the smaller ones could not match us for speed.

Today I am glad it ended that way. We could have possibly killed or maimed one of the worthless greaser scum and then had a life of arrests and law suits. Almost all of us went of to college while the greaser scum went back to their taverns, their pool halls and their crappy jobs while they were trying to get their high school equivalency tests done.

The other incedent that stands out among many of the confrantations was a party we had when we were in mid-college years. The Party was on the south side of Chicago at a girls house that we got invited to. One of our friends might have known this girl, Maria, we did not know her well. I was there with my girlfriend at that time, Reggie, and my friends Saul and Alex.

A very distant relative Joe L. was there. It was funny because at that time he had morphed himself in a Rambo type guy. He had a knife in his boot and other paraphanelia. He was also a big guy. Two of my other friends were there also, Chris and Hubert, they were twins. The party was very typical of parties at that time. The dimly lit basement, music playing, the spiked punch bowl, and some of us had our own bottles of hard liqeuer.

The party was progressing along, we were getting drunker and having a good time. More kids showed up and it was getting crowded so I went outside with my girlfriend to get some fresh air in the back yard. It was a nice warm night and we were just talking and having a nice time. Suddenly, like out of nowhere this young, blond guy approached us. He started saying something insulting, I do not remember what, but I said something back and he slapped me in the face. He was shorter and smaller and I was not versed in physical confrontations so I simply reached for him. If I had been a good street fighter I should have kicked him in the nuts and when he went down I should have then proceeded to kick the shit out of him. Today I sort of regret that my friends and I, being intelligent, never took any lessons in street fighting, we should have done it.

Reaching for this smaller jerk I found out he had a switch blade opened and was jabbing me in the stomach. So . . . I said that there was no need for violence and this was just a misunderstanding. He was nice enough not to push the confrontation and Reggie and I went back to the basement.

Meanwhile back at the party the new guy arrivals were going after our girls, the drinking continued. I went around talking to my friends telling them that these new arrivals were these German-Lithuanians from Eighteenth Street. I also saw with my friends that there might be a confrontation. After I had told my friends about the knife incedent some of our more moderate friends left the party not wanting a gang type fight. The rambo type Joe L. left with Chris and Hubert. Our group that I remember shrunk to me, Saul and Alex. The rest, there were some, but I do not remember as to who.

I went to talk to one of the bigger guys from Eighteenth Street, his name was Wolf. He felt the same way I did, there was no reason to start a fight. Fighting started in the basement anyway. I do not know how but all I know that my drunken friend Saul was swinging away at one of the newcommers. They both were drunk and flailing away at each other. Wolf and I tried to separate them and stop them when Alex, our big friend, limped in and challenged the whole group of the German-Lithuanians single handedly. They took up the challenged and all jumped on him. Saul was still flailing away at his adversary but Wolf and I were pulling the smaller guys off of Alex. Somehow the fighting stopped and we were able to get our group into cars and leave.

Later on, I believe from Chris and Hubert, who knew some of the guys from Eighteenth Street, we found out that the blond guy who almost stabbed me came back with some of his guys in his sixty one white Impala and a thirty two revolver. They were looking for us and said that they especially wanted Alex who they nicknamed as peg leg, because he had that limp.

Several weeks during that summer we would see that white Impala driving around Marquette Park looking for Alex. We avoided them and they did not seem interested in the rest of us, but only Alex was their target. We also found out from I believe Chris that these guys were a gang of hoodlums from Eighteenth Street called the Morgan Dueces. They took the name from the street in that area. The blond leader was known as a nut job because he would threaten people with the gun and was known for his extreme type behavior. We were lucky we did not push the problem with them because we would have lost against this nut job.

We continued to hear about them and one of the last stories was that they confronted one of the hoodlum local gangs called the Shy Lads. This group of jerks hung around the u-drive part of Marquette Park on the corner of 71 st and California. They were always there, sitting around like they were protecting their turf. We avoided walking or driving by that area.

This trick of avoiding confrontations was not learned by the Morgan Duece, blond jerk. The Impala drove right in on the sacred turf of the Shy Lads and of course the two jerk groups met. The Shy Lads were probably used to good Lithuanian kids who would rather run then fight. The rogue part Lithuanians, the Dueces, were completely different and surprised the Shy Lad hoodlums by the blond nut job pulling out his gun and robbing the Shy Lads of their money.

We enjoyed that story for the longest time. We were almost proud of our Lithuanians from Eighteenth Street. The Shy Lads were of the greaser types we hated.

If someone wanted a greaser type experiance they could have gone to a tavern called Hummels on 63 street. Certain nights it was filled with greaser type guys and you could smell the testasterone, the aggresive hormones. We went there to look at some nice girls and have a drink. We learned to survive in there by apologizing when one of the assholes bumped into us. The bumping was one way to start fights for them to establish their rank. When you apologized you diffused the situation.

It was a hard life for us to live in a greaser world and survive. Most of us went on to get college degrees, start families earn a good living and some of the time we crossed into the greaser world. Today I hope these macho greasers got no education, smoked all their lives and drank themselves into oblivion and suffered the frustrations of working in dead end jobs.

However we must not think that the Lithuanian community did not have our own little bunch of bully type jerks. Yes we did have our own and they were known by everyone in the community. It was always the same bunch or their hanger on types that started troubles at all of our functions. From local taverns to New Year celebrations these same jerks started fights.

My fraternity the Neo-Lithuania was very active in the sixties and always had great New Year functions and in November we also had our annual fraternity banquet. We had our own band, and our great traditions of having fun. An example was our rose waltz, where you had to buy a rose and then were allowed to ask a girl to dance that waltz. We had a great zest for life, had great friends and the fraternity was well known and respected. I was president for one year and pledge father for another. Our membership was booming and we all had great fun.

But our great functions were not imune from the bully, jerk crowd. They would always order a table for ten or twelve at our function and the during the event start some sort of trouble. As a fraternity we tried to hide the incedents and end them fast so as not to emberass our group.

Things did not get better and one New Years we decided to hire an ex-wrestler to keep the peace. You will never believe what happened that year. This bunch of hooligan jerks beat the hell out of our bouncer and threw him down the stairs, all bloody and passed out. Our ladies with the long gowns had to step over him to get to the bathroom on the lower floor. Our president was a good guy, Rimas, he got some of us together and we discussed confronting these animal and beating the hell out of them. We were all somewhat drunk but once again we have to thank God that our good role models, our own education prevented us from going out into the banquet hall, filled with over five hundred guests and start a massacre on a table full of jerks. I am sure the jerks never realized how close they came not to be pulverized.

I do not name the bully jerks here because everyone that grew up at that time knew this rotten bunch. Today, one of them is in a geriatric prison, one died recently and one is living out of the country. Those who did not grow up at that time, the names would mean nothing.

We tried to solve this ugly problem by making a black list of the jerks and not selling them a table. They tried to get the tables by using different names.

These same jerks seemed to appear at some of our pivate functions. One troubled incedent was a party at Wally's rented house in Urbana. I had graduated from there a year earlier from the College of Communications, Journalism, in advertising-marketing, and was now successfully selling toilet paper. I now had a company car, and took my girlfriend Terry and went to Wally's party in Urbana. It was super nice to see my good friends Saul and Wally.

What a great time to be had by all of us. We were young, healthy, I had a new car and money in my wallet, and a super good looking girlfriend that I was in love with. My friends were all about to graduate and get good jobs, all of their friends were there. It was a great formula for a great time at a great party.

However it was not to be so. The same rotten, stinking, jerk, bully group showed up. Somehow they must have picked up information about the party. We were dancing, drinking and having a great time. Wally had invited some Jewish guys that he knew and they were all having a great time until one of the jerks, Mazelis, walked up to one of the Jew kids and smashed him in the head. The kid went down but now Mazelis received a surprise from my friend Saul who attacked him and a fist fight ensued. They were throwing punches, wrestling until they hit the storm door and broke the glass. The fight was stopped by the other people and things calmed down but the happy mood was gone.

The jerks were not satisfied by hitting an innocent guy so now they decided they wanted to eat and raided the refrigirator. Our group of closests friends went down to the basement to make a war plan. Option one, was to go upstairs and take on the toughest guys in our community with some basement tools. We knew that the guy now in prison could pulverize several of us, so we decided on option two, and do nothing. So the party ended and everyone left. Walter had decided at that time to buy a 25 caliber gun and use it to deter any more incursions into our parties.

Everything ended well and we were lucky we did not confront these animals. We could have been killed or got lucky and killed one of the animals. That would not have been good.

It seems that young men, no matter how nice they are, will always run into jerks that can turn their world upside down. My problem was always with one of the pukes by the name of Mazelis. A smaller guy than me, dark hair, dark complexion and obsessed with my girlfriend Terry. Always making our encounters unpleasant. In the old days I would have had a duel or simply have to kill him in ambush. My last encounter with this pig dropping occured in Union Pier, Michigan. Having a great time on the beach all day long, we set up a small fire late at night on the beach and were drinking. There were only myself, Terry and my friend Iggy. It was a warm mellow night and I almost died that night.

The pig dropping George Mazelis walked out of the night and came up to our fire.

He was probably attracted again to the fact that Terry was there. He started saying something or asking something when again I showed my lack of knowledge in the world of violence. I was drunk, laying on my stomach, watching the fire when I told this garbage charecter that no one wants him here by our fire and no one likes him here and he should leave. Smart move James Bond, lay drunk on your stomach and tell your enemy what you think of him. You can imagine the predictable results. Mazelis being a soccer player saw my head as a ball and kicked me in the forehead with his sneaker type shoe. The results were devastating, I almost passed out and the force of the kick flipped me over and somehow dizzy as I was I ended up on my feet. My head hurt and I was stunned but I attacked the jerk and grappled with him. I do not know how I ended up sitting on his chest and my strong hands choking the piss out of the bastard. He was helpless and I had every intention of choking him to some end result. I did not think in terms of killing him, but simply choking and choking the bastard. It was great to see his face sputtering, swelling, turning colors and his arms flapping helplessly. Meanwhile Iggy and Terry had perceived my unintentional road to killing him, intervened to help me not commit manslaughter or maybe to save the little bastard. Iggy put on an arm lock around my neck and Terry began pulling my hair to release this piece of garbage. They saved his miserable life. Even today I wished in some small way that I could have killed this constant troublemaker.

The confrontation ended with the bastard trying to catch his breath and run away. My head hurt and I was still confused and dizzy so Terry and Iggy took me to emergency to be examined, x-rayed. The doctor told me how lucky I was. The kick could have snapped my neck and killed me. A kick to the nose would have driven the nose bone into the brain and killed me. The kick to the mouth would have broken my jaw and knocked out my teeth. So . . . I guess in that respect you could say I was lucky for simply getting kicked in the head. I could have been luckier if I could have killed the bastard for almost killing me.

This encounter shows once again how our group of nice young people were not prepared to deal with hooligan jerks. Today I believe we should have been more street wise and done things in a better way. I should have had enough brains to stand up and tell this jerk to get lost. He would not have attacked me seeing that I was bigger and my friend Iggy was also a big guy. We also could have asked him to have a drink with us and then smash a bottle into his head. Iggy could have also not pulled me off but jumped in and start smashing the guys face in and so prevent me from choking him to death. The best scenario would have been to let me finish him off as self defense. No jury would have convicted a drunk, dizzy young man fighting to protect himself from an assailent that kicked him in the head.

The next day I filed a police report and went down to the beach with a policeman, pointed George Mazelis out in the water in front of all our friends. The policeman had a sense of humor and yelled out, Georgie, Georgie, come on out of the water. The creep was very surprised as were all the onlookers. The policeman took the creep by the arm and walked him off the beach. He was put in jail and written up. I do not know how long he had to sit there but a Mr. Backaitis bailed him out. This was the father of the girl the creep was dating.

The saga continued as I waited for the trial. It seems this creep was trying to get a degree in education and an assault charge would prevent him from ever teaching. He had to spend money to do several things. First he hired a Lithuanian lawyer who kept calling me to discuss the event and find a nice solution. I should have had enough brains to realize how screwed the jerk was and ask for several thousand dollars to drop the case. At that time that money was a big sum and would have hurt the bastard and made me happy, but I was dumb.

Secondly the bastard bribed someone at the police station to steal the court file. I hope this cost him dearly. I waited and waited with my notice and nothing happened so I went to the station to find out and no one knew about my case. However I pushed until my file was put together and the trial was set again. I could see the bastards face when he got the new notices to go to trial.

Fates play a strange role in the lives of men. Drinking and stupidity mix with fates and we get what we call Karma or destiny. I always went to the Gintaras Tavern to party with my friends. I was getting drunk and happy when Mazelis showed up. I said to myself, here I go again down that slope. Mazelis walked up to me and said he is so sorry that the incedent happened. He apologized over and over and said he was drunk and did not know how it happened. He also continued to tell me how he was an orphan and had a rough life being raised by his sister. He continued to buy me drinks and I forgave him and told him I would drop the suit.

This shows how alcohol dulls the brain and how nice people become totally stupid. Here this bastard was always causing our group trouble and always confronting me because he liked my girlfriend, almost killed me and here I am drinking with him. I should have ordered a bottle of beer and have him pay for it and then smash his face with it when no one was looking, but that would not have been the real me.

One last story of our good guys running into some inbred, retarded rednecks from the Union Pier Michigan area. We were again having a nice fire on the beach with our girlfriends at night. The air was warm the stars were out, the lake was right there. We had our towels and blankets and were sipping drinks around the fire. A great time was had by all. Everyone was mellow and joking, Walter suggested we all undress and go swimming. We laughed about the suggestion because the flower children had not come on the scene yet and some of the girls still suffered from sexual repression. Walter undressed by the water and went into the lake for a swim. We continued drinking and joking when we suddenly noticed two tough looking locals approach our fire. They came up and looked at all the sharp girls and us who looked like nice polite guys. They saw that our guys were simply nice college type guys not prone to violence. They started asking us for drinks and their language became somewhat threatening. We tried to talk our way out of a confrantation but these assholes wanted to show us up for the chicken shit guys we were. None of us wanted to get up and tell these assholes to get lost.

Now the funniest thing happened because Walter had heared our conversation and silently walked up in back of these jerks completely naked and wet. Walter looked scary being six foot four, naked and wet. I believe he said something like, is there a problem here? The assholes turned around looked at this tall naked guy and lost any appetite for any confrantation.

They simple hurried away into the night and we could not stop laughing on how naked Walter scared the shit out of the inbred rednecks.

I do believe that appearance has a lot to do in striking fear into an adversary. We should have learned from that in our future run ins with the jerks.

We can see how the best of people, us, educated, good role models, nice guys almost so many times came into bad situations because of the world filled with bullies, jerks, and retards. How sorry we should feel for the good guys growing up in the ghettoes and poor neighborhoods where they are surrounded constantly by jerks and retards. What should we tell a government that wastes four trillion dollars on a useless, needless war in Iraq, orchistrated by filthy neo-cons and foreign lobbies and ignores our young people suffering in human garbage dumps?

Our College Life, First Two Years at the Navy Pier Campus

PROBABLY CLOSE TO ninety percent of DP Lithuanian young people were forced to go to college by their parents. The parents, our role models, were mostly educated, professional people that had to flee the communist, Soviet, Russian, swine, when Lithuania was grabbed up by them during WW 2. The grandparents, and the parents lost everything when they left their country. Their wealth, their careers were all lost and they all wanted to get something back through their children. They saw in their kids their own success somehow restored when the kids got a college degree.

It is not surprising that the DP kids were forced into the most challenging careers. If you check the statistics of the fifties and sixties you see mostly Lithuanian kids getting engineering degrees, medical degrees and getting great jobs, becoming leaders in large corporations.

Some of us were not cut out to be engineers and did not want to go to college. I always hated school and barely got by with very average grades of C. I perplexed the Christian Brothers who saw me stumbling around getting C's. They knew I had an IQ of 136 but my performance in all my school work was so very bad. I hated to study and only crammed for exams not to flunk. I was however so lucky to be able to get into the University of Illinois at Navy Pier. What a dump that place was, but also what a great place it was. What great opportunity was offered to us to go to the best school even if you had the most horrible high school grades. I was a C student and was given a chance to get an education. American tax dollars paid for the education by making it very affordable. America was spending tax dollars to educate their children and not wasting their money on useless, needless wars orchestrated by foreign lobbies and the so called neo-con maggots. My grades were poor and my math background did not exist, so when I went to an advisor and told him I wanted to be a physics engineer and shoot rockets, the poor man simply said that I was so far behind in math I should think of something else, perhaps. He was so right, plus I hated math.

Thinking of engineering but hating school did not seem right, but I somehow thought I could pull something off. Not getting off of that engineering track almost cost me my college career. I was forced to take science courses and one of them was Qualitative Chemistry. This course would have been very interesting for a good student but not for a nut job like me who only wanted to go out on dates and party. I had this, I believe four hour credit course with a three hour lab twice a week. The course was based on finding different elements in unknown solutions by precipitating them out or separating them out with different other elements. It was truly like detective work to find out what was in some mysterious test tube.

Our lab test was to find out what chemicals are in a test tube that was made up differently for each student. Once again I proved how dumb I can be. Instead of taking this interesting course, enjoying it, I decided to BS through the course and learn practically nothing. My misfortune was multiplied because I ended up having my nut job friend Alex in the same class. Alex of course had to have a short cut through the lab tests for unknowns. He got a book from Lithuania where his sister was studying microbiology which explained that you can find unknowns in a liquid by dipping a platinum wire in the unknown and then sticking it into a flame. The color of the flame then can tell you what element is in your unknown. Well this goofy test, plus my attitude toward education, and having an ignorant foreigner professor all made up a perfect storm for blowing me out of college. My dumb test, with the wire, caused me to list a group of elements in my unknown that were wrong, and the dumb ass professor Savoy deducted something for each wrong answer, so the fool professor Savoy gave me a test grade for an important lab test, a minus 180. Now you have to understand how dumb that grade is when you get on your test a minus 180. There is no way to average that minus grade into a passing grade. So if I got three 90's in my hourly lecture classes and average them out I would still have a grade of 22 and would flunk the class. So . . . here we can see where I was condemned by this foreigner, ignorant Professor Savoy to get tossed out of college because he was so stupid and did not know how to grade tests. The only thing dumber than the ignorant dumb assed professor in this incident was me. I should not have accepted a minus 180 as a lab grade and calmly walked over to the Dean's office and demanded a legitimate zero for my grade instead of living with a minus 180. If a student turns in a test or term paper that has a lot of mistakes, the number of mistakes reduce the grade where the student eventually gets a zero grade. You never go into negative numbers in marking tests.

If I had gotten a zero grade I would have been able to average out a humble C grade for Qualitative Analysis. However the silly bastard gave me a D which put me on probation the next semester. I had to get a 3.8 grade average next semester to get off probation. This grading is based on a 5 point system.

If we see a C is worth three, a B is worth 4 and an A is worth 5, I had to get almost all B's and an A to average out any C, that I might get. My problem was that I was a C student.

So I signed up for some easier courses like psychology, geography, but I was still stuck with my cursed German class, a sure C. So I went to talk to all my teachers about how I have to get an A or B in their class to stay in college. I remember only talking to my geography teacher, a senile old biddy, who told me that God is perfect and so he can get an A. She is the teacher and deserves a B, the rest of us, who knows. As a parting shot the biddy stated that she does not like students who chew gum in front of her, I was chewing gum.

I believe I also took philosophy at that time and biology 101. I was scared this time. I was out of tricks this time. I was ready to hit the books seriously this time for the first time in my life. I worked hard and was rewarded by praises from my philosophy professor who told me to try to time the speed of my thought process to my ability to write essay type answers. The biology professor would make comments during the two hour tests by saying, "there goes Mr. Krumplis leaving in only one hour, I guess I made the test too easy". It was funny how I got to like biology and was so good at it that I screwed up the curve type grading system for the desperate pre med students. Higher grades forced the curve grading system to be pushed up higher and made poorer grades harder to be improved by the curve grading method.

Biology lab tests were even more humorous because we had to move from different tables, look through different microscopes and explain different exhibits. As an example you would look through a microscope and see a pointer pointing at a nucleus of a cell and check of the answer as, nucleus. However the desperate, insanely competitive pre med students would move the pointer to a different location and all the students following the bastard that made the change would get the answer wrong. The professor figured out this scam and did not set up such exhibits.

One of my most interesting biology test exhibits was a wire inserted diagonally through a cat's skeleton. You had to name everything the wire pierced, all the covering tissues of all the organs and all the organs. This was a real mind bender for all the desperate pre med students. It was always fun to watch the desperate pre med students clawing, pushing, falling over to see the sheets of grades being posted on the walls.

The other course that concerned me was my German course, that I knew, I would only get a C. Both of my German teachers were old Jewish biddies that I believed had communist leanings. I got into an argument with one of them about the pro commie books we had to read. One of them was about a nuclear scientist spying for the Soviets, he was portrayed as an idealist. The book was called, Das Kalte Light. I asked the professor why we had to read this commie type book when German literature was filled with so many good books. The professor biddy told me that perhaps I was paranoid and saw a commie under every rock. I answered by telling her that maybe there was a commie under every rock in America.

My German final came up and I was a nervous wreck. I got lucky however and it might have been a small, lucky encounter, that saved my college career. I met a girl I knew, Aukse, or Goldie, who had just taken the German Final from our group but on a different schedule and she told me what was on the test. The hard part was a huge paragraph you had to translate to English. The paragraph was from a political speech that was given by Dean Rusk to the people of Berlin. You can imagine how I would have not done well on this because of the complexity of political thought and long sentences.

I rushed to the library and not being well versed in research was frustrated in locating this speech. By a miracle I found this speech and that particular paragraph in English. I memorized and memorized that big paragraph until I could recite it.

The final came and I stumbled through the easy parts and then smiled when I saw the same paragraph. I breezed right through with the translation and that saved my college career possibly. I could laugh now how I suffered through those German classes. I had to give in German, in one class, a speech about the human circulatory system and made the other students laugh so hard that they had tears in their eyes, yet here I was beating them all out with my perfect translation.

My next worry was the crazy biddy in geography. The final had one huge section that she wanted us to explore some geographical concept, ask a question and answer it. My mind screamed, huh, what? I was confused but since I was well versed in bullshit, I posed a question. Why not dam the desert rivers, the Tigris and the Euphrates and continue the dams to join both dams and create a huge inland lake to irrigate the huge arid lands around that area. I was concerned about the test but then when we discussed our tests in class this wonderful old biddy could not stop praising my whole idea of creating an inland lake. She also said that the other students asked such boring question that they should have asked in class or known from our text books. I lucked out again and got a good grade that helped me get off the probation.

There were other problems at Navy Pier that I had to overcome. One of the biggest was my horrible attitude for studying, if that fact was not enough to kill my college career, I also had other problems, I drank a lot and dated a lot. Now if all that was not enough, I fell madly in love with a German girl Erica, her name should have been erotica. I met her in one of my classes and that was the end. We could not hang up the phones when we got home from school. She had blond hair, a cute face and a body to turn you instantly to stone. I and she were so in love, that I told my dad I was thinking of getting married. Well . . . this announcement went over like huge fart during a prayer session. My dad, who was the nicest father anyone could imagine having, told me to pack my bags and leave home. Huh . . . I was not even twenty one, with no suitcases to pack my junk in, no money, and no job. I had to call Erica and tell her we can not get married just now. So ended my first great love affair.

After two years at University of Illinois, Navy Pier I left for the Urbana campus and a different life with different girls. Erica dropped out of school and married some lucky sailor. I do not think that marriage lasted but I never saw Erica again.

There were other problems at Navy Pier. There were mandatory courses that we had to take. I think they were there to flunk out kids. In the beginning of the semester the narrow halls of the Pier were so crowded that it was hard to get from one end to the other during the ten minutes to switch classes. At the end of the semester the halls were fairly empty. So many kids were allowed to register that there were mandatory killer classes that were there to get rid of the huge surplus of kids. This destructive system was there for all four semesters that I went there.

I was well aware of one of these killer classes that scared me. It was called Rhetoric, a mandatory class. It consisted of writing perfect composition papers. One error or two and you got a C, a few more and you gut a D and ended up on probation. These courses culled out the student population. You were either prepared to write on a college level or you were not and got kicked out. Here the high school kids that had good English teachers survived and the ones that had bad English teachers got kicked out of college. I went to a prestigious high school, De La Salle. A Christian Brothers school, it was good because it thought you to be a good person. The problem for me was that my four years of English was thought by the same teacher, a Mr. Lew, a big fat man. This man cared nothing if we learned anything. He was, the most lazy uncaring teacher, and a perfect one for me, because I did not want to learn anything. During class he would punish the same pathetic clowns by having them come up and sit on his lap. He said this was his punishment method for bad children, they had to come up, as he said and sit on daddy's lap. Much later I found out that he was a flaming faggot, a queer, and had the kids sit on his lap for that reason. That was bad enough in itself, but his lack of having any desire to teach us English grammar cost some kids a college education.

I can not believe that I had this queer giving me useless education and that a hundred Christian brothers that worked with him did not know it. Today I am not supposed to call him queer but refer to him simply as a bad gay teacher who did nothing bad by making innocent boys sit on his lap and thought me nothing for four years.

I do not want to knock my old school, I had some great teachers that tried to get me to be a good student. A brother Basil knew my IQ and was my home room teacher, he said, why not try to do the best by using your brains, and know you can do it, and then go back and stumble around with your very average grades.

I have digressed here and want to get back to my rhetoric course. I had troubles with it, and was worried. I went to see a Doctor Runyon, my teacher, to discuss my problems. He asked me a few questions about grammar and I did not even know at this time, what an adverb was. He saw my problem and I am glad he was a fair and intelligent man and not like the idiot chemistry teacher Savoy or those crazy old biddies. Doctor Runyon said that it was too late for me to learn grammar while I was in his class. He told me that because I spoke correctly, I should write the way I spoke and things would turn out ok. I got a C in rhetoric from him and was very happy with it. He might have felt sorry for me perhaps and was more lenient in grading my papers, maybe.

There was another interesting aspect at Navy Pier and that was that Physical Education courses were mandatory and forced all the out of shape, obese, fat asses to do physical exercises and get in shape. Today the big mommy government would argue that the college had no right to force people to improve their physical condition. That is why today America is filled with so many morbidly obese fat asses and our health care is overwhelmed by the problems they develop.

We of course did not like this mandatory physical education requirement. It started in the first semester and you had to take a physical condition type test. You had to do so many sit ups, push ups, chin ups and if you failed you were forced to take a physical conditioning class. If you passed at the end of the course then next semester you were able to choose something more interesting. The test was interesting in the fact that you had to climb a thick rope and touch the top of the rope about twenty or thirty feet high. I can imagine today such a test would surely be banned by the fear of law suits.

I passed the first semester and ended up taking wrestling in the next. During an exhibition match I refused to be flipped on my back and some of my ribs were broken off from my sternum. So . . . everyone heard the crack and I was able to sit out the rest of the semester simply observing and writing some reports. I got a passing grade and it never entered my head that I could have possibly sued this great college with endangering me.

My last two PE courses were, boating and fishing and archery. The boating and fishing started with canoeing lessons in Lake Michigan, right next to Navy Pier. This was truly a beautiful experience, the lake, the Chicago skyline, and us bobbing around in nice canoes.

One incident I can never forget was my poor friend Alex coming late for this class and not dressed in proper type clothes but wearing a suit and tie and trying to step off of the cement wall into a canoe. We were watching this from our canoes when Alex slipped and fell into the lake between the canoe and the cement wall. Then a feat of strength I had never imagined occurred. The instructor reached down to struggling Alex and picked him up out of the water by grasping his wrists and set him down on solid ground. I believe Alex could have weighed up to two hundred and fifty pounds. We all felt sorry for Alex and no one laughed.

The fishing part of the course consisted of casting lures at targets on the floor from different distances. We did this when we could not go canoeing. The last semester was Archery, it was easy and fun, all we did was try to hit the center of the targets to get a good grade.

The encompassing problem at the Navy Pier campus was that education was so cheap and the entrance rules were so low that the huge number of students at the beginning of each semester was overwhelming the system. So . . . they gave almost everyone a chance for a college education but then set high limits to select out only college material. This reduced the numbers tremendously as people realized they were either too stupid, too unprepared, unmotivated or what ever else. As I said before, the narrow hallway of the Pier was fairly empty after about the middle of the semester.

There were many other reasons students failed, but among the Lithuanians it was the simple ethnic symptom of bonding together. We had three tables at one end of the cafeteria where we congregated. Any time of day, if you went there, you always found some Lithuanians to talk to. The classes you took sometimes had an hour or three before the next class. So you spent that time with your friends. You talked, or you had lunch, or you started playing cards. Card playing was big at our three tables. You sometimes missed class because you were playing cards. Some students missed so many classes and played cards so much that they flunked out.

In summary we can say we lived in a completely different world. Education was affordable and everyone, rich, poor, dumb, smart had a chance to grab on to the American Dream. Everything depended on you if you could hold on to that dream or not.

Last Two Years of College at the Urbana U of I Campus

THE NEXT TWO years at the Urbana Campus were the same as my first two years at the Navy Pier campus, I drank too much, hated to study, was obsessed with girls, loved pranks and never grew up. I was like a weird Peter Pan, a man child. I must have never heard of maturity.

I was forced to make some decisions at this point. The university asked me to chose a curriculum and a degree that I wanted to earn. This was difficult for me because I did not like any studying. I went for counseling and found out that physics and math were not in my stars. I took a test for possibly studying to be an architect but did very badly on spatial perception. What to do, what to pick, huh? Well I thought and thought and realized that all my life I was good as a salesman. I finally figured out I should study advertising, marketing and make use of my people skills. The College of Communications, offered three branches of study, news writing, radio TV, and advertising-marketing. I chose the advertising-marketing branch and started taking a mix of business related courses and the artsy type ad courses. This should have been interesting, challenging but it was not.

My roommate Alex in one semester of my last two years of college in Urbana

I did what I always did, ignored my studies and term papers until the last two weeks of the semester, and then took Dexedrin, coffee, and other concoctions to stay awake for two weeks, and catch up on months of notes and readings. The zombie state I was in toward the end of my finals always made me say, I will never do this again.

During the semester break I went back home to recuperate and my parents always thought I had some terrible disease because of the way I looked.

I had tried to change my study habits but failed all the time, because of the distractions. The roommates, the guys in the dorm, the girls, the weekends, all conspired to distract me from study.

I had interesting roommates each semester. My friend Alex was a roommate for part of one semester, we almost ended up killing each other. Alex had worse study habits then mine, if that can be imagined. He would almost never sleep, or sleep during the day. He would constantly come in at all hours of the night, slam the doors, put on the lights and wake me up. He did not have the common sense to go study or read in the lounge. On top of all that irritation his feet smelled so bad that the smell traveled out through the vent above the door, filled the corridor that about fifty feet from our door there was a double corridor door and when another of my friends, Wally, would enter our area he would know that Alex had taken off his shoes in our room. This is not an exaggeration.

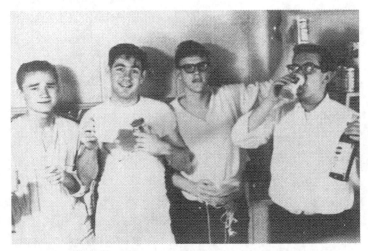

In our dorm room in Snyder house we are getting drunk again. Third guy from left is my roommate Sandy.

It was a bad situation because I could not go without sleep with Alex waking me up all the time and my friend Wally hated Alex for some reason. The problem with Alex and Wally exploded in a restaurant where we were all at. One word led to another and we barely avoided a physical confrontation. It ended with unbelievable shouting and name calling. Wally kept calling Alex a peg leg and Alex nicknamed Wally at that time as a sub-cretin.

This particular roommate situation ended when I threatened Alex about waking me up at all hours and he responded to my threats that he would inject the oranges I had in my room with all kinds of bacteria he had available in his microbiology class. I went to our floor monitor and told him that Alex was nuts and wanted to kill me. The graduate student in charge of us was smart enough to move Alex out to a different room and I was left by myself.

My next roommate was a guy by the name of Sandy. Tall, blond, good looking ex-fraternity guy. He came from a rich family out east and lived in a fraternity house here in U of I. Something happened to him that he had to leave the frat house. I never found out if he ran out of money or something else got him out.

We got along really well. He had money, I had very little. He would always invite me to go for pizza or beer and pay for it. He looked at all of us, independents, as if we were known by the fraternities and sororities as something as lesser type critters. The fraternities were the elite. According to him we should have all aspired to become fraternity type people.

We became good friends and Sandy tried to make me look like a frat guy. According to him I did not look like the college type. My haircut was wrong, my clothes were wrong, so today I would have been faced with a complete makeover. Sandy never let up on his frat praises and told me how the girls loved the frat guys so much because they might get some frat pin from the guy. He told me about his girlfriend, Portia, I thought an odd name, and how this girl was madly in love with him. I never met her, I wonder why?

Sandy was rich and spoiled and could not discipline himself to get up in time for tests or classes. He asked me constantly to wake him up in the mornings but he had the hardest time getting out of bed. It was so ridiculous that I would shoot him with a water pistol in the morning to irritate him into getting up. He was a good considerate roommate and we became friends. I invited him to visit my home in Chicago during one of the breaks, he lived in Boston and did not want to go there during the break. He must have been amazed how humbly we lived in the small apartment, a second floor unit in a bungalow.

Sandy talked always about the greatness of the fraternities, Their elite standings in society, their connections to top people. Wally and I would listen to his bullshit and one day it all added up for us. Sandy did not study engineering, science, or business, but studied political science. Now here was an example of our government worker and our politician. It was clear for us why the government was always having problems.

I believe today the government problem has become so great that it threatens our way of life. The problem of today began many generations ago because government work and political careers became infested with bullshit type people. We can ask ourselves about the percentages of engineers, scientists, businessmen in our government versus the political science students and the blood sucking lawyers. So we develop a government infected by the bull shitters and then we get a choice to vote for different bull shitters or lawyers. While these type of people are slowly destroying our country we believe we have some sort of choice to repair America.

I wished I had kept in touch with him. I am sure with his good looks, his money, he found some lucrative government job.

The next roommate was Marty. He was Jewish, but we got along real nice. Marty was studying accounting. We never talked much nor became friends. We only had one incident which was unpleasant but I settled it real quick and we got along after that point. I was sleeping one night when Marty came home from somewhere in the middle of the night and turned on his big stereo system full blast. The record playing was about car races and the main sound was a bunch of Ferraris revving up. I was popped out of my deep sleep with this horrendous noise. I could not believe that someone would be that inconsiderate, and obnoxious to do that in the middle of the night to a sleeping person. I was very upset, and when I could control myself I simply told him that if he ever did that again the stereo would never work again. He understood that I would render the stereo unworkable by making some adjustments. I want to give Marty the benefit of doubt that he was drunk or did not think, but he was not being an obnoxious Jew.

Marty and I had a very strange roommate relationship. We never got to know one another or even cared to now one another. We never went out to get a beer or pizza. The only great thing that happened having had Marty for a roommate was that through him I met a lifelong friend, Bruce. Bruce and I became friends. We played many chess games, went out for beer and pizza, and drove around in his 140 or 150 Jaguar sports car. I loved those cars but always heard how Bruce was always fixing them. Bruce was a great prankster and one day we took his girlfriend Mitzi to a local country green grass carnival. Mitzi went where we took her and in that carnival there was a nudie strip show in a large tent. The tent was filled with red neck farmer types and when we walked in with a girl there were whistles and other noises. Mitzi had no idea the girls would undress completely and covered her face when the girls took everything off. Fun and laughter was had by all except Mitzi.

Bruce and I, with Mitzi, explored the rest of the carnival games. Bruce found a table with a huge tub of water and a bunch of floating plastic yellow ducks. The wall was covered with prizes for someone who would pull out a duck with numbers on it. We wanted to get Mitzi a prize so we started paying a quarter for looking at each duck. There were no prizes to be got so Bruce decided to pull out the rest of the ducks and show the operator that all of them were not numbered. What saved us at that time was that the operator was much smaller than Bruce. Bruce was a big guy over six feet tall and heavy set. The operator started yelling for help from the rest of the trickster operators and we saw men beginning to move toward us. Bruce grabbed Mitzi and we rushed to the Jaguar and got out of the carnival. I always wanted to ask Bruce what he thought would happen if you started exposing a carnival game in the carnival.

Bruce had some stay awake pills from a friend of his, whose mother was a doctor. We played chess for the pills and I am sure they helped me stay awake for the last two weeks of the semester to get passing grades.

Our friendship evolved further as I was disciplinarian of the floor and had to maintain order on the floor. I could give out tickets to noise makers but my tickets had to have a witness signing on for the complaint to go to student court. It was difficult for me to get witnesses against big PE majors or simply just big guys. You can imagine a little guy signing a complaint against some big trouble making jerk, and then one morning finding himself in the big public shower with the same big jerk. There was one scary big jerk, Murphy, whom I ticketed and Bruce counter signed. Murphy finally got tossed out of the dorms but for some other infraction not my tickets. If it were for my tickets I would never have taken another shower.

To show what a prankster, trouble maker, this Murphy guy was I have one little story. Our University Administration wanted to civilize us and socialize us by making us have a common lunch in our cafeteria on Sundays with girls from the dorms across the street.

This attempt started out badly even before the girls got to the cafeteria. They had to walk along side of our building to get to the cafeteria and the guys on all the floors by the big windows were mooning the girls and exposing themselves to the girls as they walked by. The girls were horrified looking at all the obscenity.

They looked so nice dressed in their Sunday best, they possibly wanted to meet some nice guys while eating a nice lunch. They were greeted instead by sex starved maniacs who were sexually repressed by the rules of the University. Having studied psychology, having been sexually repressed by the University I can safely say it was the Administrations fault that the young men acted so obscenely.

I have digressed here but anyway back to the cafeteria and Murphy. As lunch progressed and we were served mashed potatoes, beef and brown gravy, Murphy started making loud noises while eating. He was slurping, coughing and attracted every ones attention, when the audience of viewers was large he would shove his face into the gravy and mashed potatoes pulling out pieces of beef and making loud pig noises, then shove the food in his mouth with his hands. This was truly funny for the guys but the girls were filled with disgust. I could not ticket him in the cafeteria.

One of my other roommates was a guy by the name of Wallace. He was from one of the small towns in Illinois. A real American guy from a small town, I think he was overwhelmed about living in the dorms and college life.

University of Illinois, Urbana, in front of our dorm, Snyder House. Roommate Wallace on the left, me on the right, alcohol is king.

Who has time to study when there are trees to climb and alcohol. This is in front of Snyder House. Wallace is in the tree, I am on the right.

We got along really well, we respected each other and always tried to study in the lounges as not to upset the sleep of the roommate. We never became friends because he did not party or drink. He was very naïve about sex and the girls' genitals. It was funny to me that he knew nothing about a subject that was tearing me apart. I had my walls plastered with Playboy pinups and at that time only breasts were allowed to be shown but no pubic hair, that would have been a sin according to God and some withered old religious freaks. We got along well and one day he said I need a big favor from you, my parents are coming to visit me and could you for that weekend remove the naked girls from your wall. Of course I agreed and took off all the nudie pictures.

I finally broke our code of being a good roommate. It was not my intention to do this but circumstances forced me to impose on my roommate a great unpleasantness. The unpleasantness was my old ex-roommate, Alex.

The saga of Alex must be told in sequence to understand his comings and goings. After our breakup as roommates Alex moved to a Catholic dorm called Newman Hall. He had a roommate from India. This arrangement had to be strange because Alex kept the same hours as with me. Coming and going when ever he felt.

One night he had played bridge all night and went to sleep at 5:30 AM and the Indian thought he had been sleeping all night wanted to wake him up at six AM. He put a large alarm clock by his ear and woke him up. Well Alex got up and started beating up the Indian. After the fight the director of Newman Hall had to find other roommates for the two fighters. Alex found some fool that would room with him but no one wanted to room with the Indian. So the end result was that both had to leave Newman Hall. Alex got his refund check for room and board. He now had to find a place to live. So what was the problem?

Problems sometimes multiply for smart people that are crazy. Alex was a giant magnet for trouble. Driving back to Chicago with his parent's car he was racing, passing and driving like he always drove, irresponsibly. So . . . he had an accident and ended up spending the refund check to repair the car, but now he was broke and nowhere to live. To understand about his driving I would like to mention two other incidents in his life related to driving. At one time Alex had a convertible Dodge Coronet and came around offering us rides to show his great new car. Driving or cruising around we would end up next to some young guy stopped at the lights and it took Alex one second of eye contact to challenge the guy to a drag race when the light turned green. Alex had an automatic transmission in the convertible and was convinced that you could put the car in park, race the engine, and slam the gear into drive. We all told him you can not do this to an automatic transmission. He said he read the manual and that a Dodgematic transmission could handle that. So . . . he kept drag racing until one day he had no car and told us the transmission is being repaired for big dollars.

His next driving incident was truly fantastic. He was now married and his wife was with him. He was on some expressway when a driver on his left cut in front of him to get to an exit. This upset Alex so bad that he put the car into four wheel drive, turned hard right, hit the curb, humped on the grass and raced uphill to catch the guy who had cut him off. He had to go up the grass because he had missed the exit that the culprit used. The police spotted this unbelievable chase and Alex pointed to the vehicle in front and signaled for the cops to chase it. After the culprit was chased down by the cops and Alex, they asked him, what had the man done. Alex explained to the cops that the asshole had cut him off to get to the exit. You can understand how dumb the cops felt, so they gave Alex a bunch of different tickets. His wife threatened divorce if he ever did that again. She had smashed her head when the car jumped the curb.

Anyway back in Urbana Alex has no money and nowhere to live. So . . . he comes to his old friend, me, for help. At this time I had been elected as disciplinarian of our floor. My job was to maintain peace and quiet on my floor. I was permitted to give out tickets to noise makers and bring them to student court. I also had the keys to the first floor lounges. Alex could not survive living in all night fast food eateries so I would let him into the lounges to sleep on the couches.

This worked out for a while and after breakfast I would smuggle him some crackers and milk from the cafeteria. This worked for a while but people using the lounges started asking me who was the bum with stinking feet I let into our lounges every night. Alex had a very heavy dark beard that would require him almost two times a day to shave to look well groomed. Well with no place to wash, no place to shave he started to look like a derelict bum. I was getting too many questions about the bum in the lounges and so had to come up with another plan.

I talked to my nice roommate Wallace and told him about my distant relative Alex and the problem of him sleeping in the lounges. Wallace had classes in late morning and I had early classes, so he said if I left early I could let Alex sleep in my bed in the morning. This was ok for a while but the stinking feet got in the way again. The stench was so bad that it would wake Wallace up from sound sleep. We tried washing the feet, using powders, but nothing worked. The solution we worked out was that Alex would not remove his shoes while Wallace was in the room.

Alex finally got some money and moved out somewhere, I do not care where, he was not my problem anymore.

I had one other roommate, a black guy, who was very nice and we got along well. He was a small guy, light skinned for a black guy. He was very quiet and never seemed to be there. I think he was always in the lounges or the library. One day I noticed he had a ring shaped like a belt buckle, I told him it was very nice and he gave it to me. You figure that one out. His name I only remember as being something like Boady. My room, our room, was always busy, I had many friends. The floor guys always stopped in, my Lithuanian friends stopped by, I had visitors on weekends. So . . . after several months of having this nice roommate he disappeared one day. He, and his belongings were gone from the room. I never found out why or where he went. Maybe it was one of those alien abductions.

So much for all my roommates, They were all nice except for Alex. The guys on our floor where all nice guys except, for Murphy, who was nuts. Most of the guys were from small towns and it was interesting to talk to them because they had very limited exposures compared to DP guys like me.

Born in Lithuania, living under communist swine occupation, then living under Nazi occupation then running from the communist animals and hiding from US bombs at the end of the war in Germany. Our conversations were great mental exercises, covering history, economics, God, we all thought at that time we knew all the answers and defended our views. We sat around smoking pipes, cigars and acting very intellectual, sometimes.

Our floor was known as the Snyder Spiders, and we thought we were cool. Our world in the early sixties was very innocent. Drugs had not arrived at the scene yet, the flower children had not come to our campus yet, we were still hopelessly sexually repressed and controlled by administrations that were influenced by a bunch of shriveled, old religious zealots, the Taliban of America at that time. It is funny today, fifty years later, we are fighting the same type of religious freak zealots, called Taliban in Afghanistan. I suppose fifty years from now these religious freaks will also vanish in Afghanistan.

Sexual repression existed because the pill was not available, the church had a monopoly of disseminating their bullshit at the pulpit, there was no internet to counter their weekly propaganda and the entertainment field was controlled by censorship run by the zealot American Taliban. Add abortion which was deemed a sin and forbidden, abortions could only be performed in dark closets and basements for big payments to criminal doctors. So . . . the young people were forced into servile masturbation by a religious society.

Imagine a censorship so powerful that pubic hair on nudes had to be air brushed out and that if one pubic hair showed on any one picture you had, you could be arrested.

It was humorous to see how young people tried to find sexual release. I dated girls from LAR residence halls, this was Lincoln Avenue Residence halls. The rules for girls were strict and they were locked up on weekdays at ten PM and Saturdays, Sundays, a few hours later. Minutes before the closing hour the young people were making out in the lounge areas, telephone booths for the lucky ones, and any alcove that provided some privacy. I am surprised that the religious freaks did not appoint some shriveled old biddy with a cattle prod to try to separate the young couple from their embraces and pathetic dry humping. If the girl was locked out at the closing hour I guess she had to sleep outside or some other place. She could not go to the men's dorm, that was forbidden. The results of these sexual repressions and rules resulted in massive masturbation and the so called fantastic wet dreams guys suffered or enjoyed.

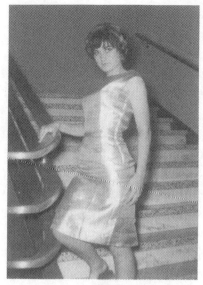

My girlfriend Sharon in Urbana.

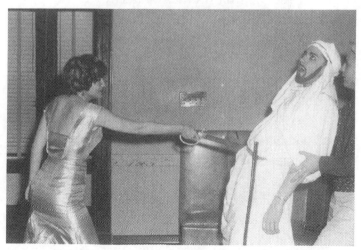

Sharon and I clowning around at a masquerade party.

This sexual repression constantly hounded us on campus. One evening I went to a costume party with a very nice girlfriend, Sharon, she was wearing a gold type sexy dress and I was dressed as an Arab with a white head wrap, a white cape and a large saber type real sword I had in my belt, I had also painted on my face a very black beard. We were heading back after the party walking through some area where there were some bushes near a building so we decided to hide in the bushes and make out a little bit. As we were playing around, some Taliban guard must have heard us and started crawling through the bushes to investigate possibly a sin. It was a dark night and this idiot was coming for us through the bushes with his flashlight. I did not now who was coming after us, so I simply was holding the sword in my hand when this old guardian of virtue put the light on my face and saw my getup and sword and became speechless. I should have screamed some Arab war cry and this old shit would have died. He finally gathered his wits about him and asked us what we were doing in the bushes. We told him we were just talking and had left a costume party. We had broken no laws and it was not past curfew for girls so he had nothing on us. He told us to go on home and we did not argue. We should have challenged the old shit security guard and asked him to leave us alone and get lost. We were however conditioned to accept all kinds of repressions and acted like sheep.

Pity the gay person at that time. It would have been better to be branded a witch, a ghoul or a cannibal. These people were known a queers and perverts or lesbians and there was zero acceptance for these fellow humans. The word gay was not introduced until later. I would like to bring up only one example of how these poor people were treated. One night I came back to the dorms sexually frustrated from heavy petting and saw all the guys running around all the floors like they had lost all their minds. Everyone was running to one side of the building and crowding into rooms to look across the center courtyard into a window where two gay guys were making out on the lower floor room. These unfortunates had forgotten to close the shades. I think if Christ or the devil had appeared in our courtyard it would not have created such an audience.

It ended sadly, the two gay guys were hounded out of the dorm by telephone calls, banging on their doors, threats of all kinds. From this we can see the attitude toward sex of any kind at that time. Sex was only allowed after some shriveled or pedophilic priest blessed your marriage and then allowed you to procreate as the state still made sure that oral and anal sex was against the law. I wonder how happy God was with these results of religious repression done in his name.

Some of the guys from small towns felt an unbelievable amount of freedom from their small minded communities. They became free spirits. One of them was a guy by the name of Quail. Nice young man that wanted to be challenged to do anything. We challenged him to run long distances. We would drive him out of town twenty or more miles and he would always return to the dorm.

Our floor was filled with pranksters also and that made my job as disciplinarian interesting. One of the bad ass pranks was to fill one whole room with wrinkled up newspapers, When a student went home for the weekend, or both guys went home the other guys would get into the room and fill it from floor to ceiling, and wall to wall with balled up newspapers. The guys coming back from a weekend at home, late at night, and having homework to do would open their door and see the doorway blocked with balled up newspapers. The yelling would start and I had to silence them. It was hard not to laugh as they struggled to remove the papers from the whole room.

The other prank everybody had suffered from was being penciled in to your room. The doors of our rooms were of solid wood and opened inward. So . . . at night we locked our doors when we went to sleep to prevent some drunk coming into the wrong room. This locking of the door allowed the prankster to push the top third of the door inward and drop a pencil between the door and the jamb. The harder he pushed, the further the pencil dropped, this action caused unbelievable pressure on the lock mechanism. It was impossible to turn the knob from the inside, you were trapped. There were only two ways to get out, one was to call for help and have someone push the door again and try to pick the pencil out from the outside. The next method was to kick the door real hard at the spot were the pencil was. Sometimes this worked by crushing the pencil and easing the pressure on the lock.

Speaking of doors another story comes to mind I call the Tucky Door Story. Tuckey was a big guy on our floor. He was either an athlete or PE major. Someone had spotted Tuckey in a far away canteen having some coffee with a girl. So . . . the guys decided it would be fun to pick his lock and remove his heavy wooden door and carry to the far away canteen and give Tucky the door. This was done, the guys walked into the canteen carrying the heavy door, walked up to Tuckey's table and gave him his door.

The story ended well. Tucky had to drag the door back by himself but was super pissed. He yelled, shouted and I had to tell him to keep it down. He threatened harm to the pranksters until they told him they would not give him the hinge pins to put his door back. He had to promise to forgive them if they gave him the pins. He got the pins and everybody went to sleep, case closed.

There was no end to pranks. One of the funniest was when card games were organized in some rooms and the door was locked to everyone else. The pranksters got lighter fuel and squirted it under the door. The players never noticed this until the fuel was lit and the flames erupted in their room. This was safe because the flames were instantly stamped out by the card players. The tile on the floor and the door never had a chance to be damaged by the surface type flames of the fuel. This was a good one because it sure scarred the hell out of the card players, yet caused no damages.

Another prank that was fun to watch was done when the girls came to our cafeteria on Sundays. We would start smuggling out those cellophane packages of crackers out of the cafeteria and in our rooms make small slits with razors in the packages. We would then write all kinds of obscenities and ugly notes and stick them back in the packages. Then on Sundays we would go in earlier to the cafeteria and dump all our message filled crackers on top of the cracker container. Now all we had to do is watch the cute girls pick up some crackers and start finding the messages, this was great to watch because the girls erupted with laughter and giggles when they found the messages. It was even more fun when they crushed the crackers and put the whole thing in the soup and fished the paper out with their spoon and then read the message, a truly clever prank that hurt no one.

The next trick was painful to the recipients. Here a thirty five gallon plastic garbage can was filled with water and leaned up against the victim's door. This was not enough to wait for the poor guy to open the door and get thirty five gallons of water in his room, the pranksters added a long string of firecrackers taped to the barrel with a cigarette fuse. The fuse worked simply by inserting the fuse into the middle of the cigarette and lighting the cigarette. The cigarette burned down to the fuse and then the fuse ignited giving the pranksters plenty of time to get to their rooms and wait for the shit to hit the fan. Simply put what happened was easy to predict. The first firecrackers to explode brought the victim to the door to see who dared to disturb him, as he yanked the door open inwardly the remaining firecrackers and the thirty five gallons of water spilled into his room. It scared the hell out of the victims in the room, you had plenty of exploding firecrackers and thirty five gallons of water in your room. Cursing, yelling, and explosions brought me out of the room to do my job as disciplinarian. Seeing what has happened I could not write any tickets, you can not blame the victim. This particular trick was played on victims that have somehow pissed someone off. It could have been the victim was snobbish or studied too much. The clean up part for the victim was the worst part of this prank.

The cigarette fuse trick was also played on the guys on the second floor who called the floor the Vrimja floor or something like that. Most of them were Jews and I think their clannish actions pissed of some of our pranksters and they would set of huge firecrackers with the delayed fuse inside their corridors. This always ended up with the victims running up and down stairs looking as to who threw the firecracker inside their hallway. They never learned about the delayed fuse.

Not all incidents were inside the dorms, when we had some snow we would get a bunch of independent guys and walk up to some frat house and fling a few snowballs at their windows and doors. We hid most of the guys out of sight with a bunch of snowballs and when the frat guys, few in number, confronted us we would rush our huge numbers out of hiding and bury them and their doorway with snowballs. This was always fun to whip these arrogant frat guys who always believed they were better than us.

One other famous prank was the University well known water fights. I never was in one on campus and could not describe it. I heard about them and read about them. They start with guys opening up fire hydrants and splashing any people walking by. Any cars driving by would get splashed and this prank spread from street to street. The bad part here was that the rowdies would grab other students and toss them into the huge pools of water or into the actual funnels of water coming out of the hydrants. This was fun until the tossed victims landed on hydrants and cement and got hurt.

The administration knew what time of year the prank would start and gave orders to all the teachers to go out and sit on fire hydrants the moment trouble started. This traditional water fight was nipped in that way.

I was in a water fight on our floor that started in the most weird way. Someone squirted someone with a hypodermic needle through a vent above the door. The victim came back with a glass of water and tossed it at the initiator. This multiplied when other guys started tossing bigger cups and other containers at each other. Soon it was a mass of yelling guys running around with all different containers of water. The corridors where full of water and the bathroom was used to fill up the containers, everything would have ended well accept for the fact that someone called the building manager who came around the corner of the hall and ran into one of our fighters dragging a thirty five gallon garbage can partially filled with water. The fighting ended with a sermon and the poor guy with the big container of water got tossed out of the dorm. It was a lot of fun, accept for our fellow friend who got tossed.

There were many other incidents that were humorous on campus. Sometimes the humor part was at the expense of some poor student. One such incident occurred on the second floor of Gregory Hall during class break when we had to go to different rooms for different courses.

I have to give some history of campus life to show how this incident could occur. The government and the university had become aware of the need to make education accessible to crippled and blind people. Ramps were made to buildings, curbs were leveled for wheel chairs and many other things were done to help these young people get an education. I guess this had to be done because prayers did not work.

I tried to organize a branch of our fraternity Neo-Lithuania in Urbana. This is one of our meetings. Sitting left N. Grybauskaite, R. Merkelyte, A. Paplenaite, V. Aleksandriunaite. Standing left: V. Bylaitis, R. Sosyte, R. Raulinaityte, me.

The incident I want to describe was horribly sad yet it had a humorous side. There was a young man, a paraplegic, I believe, he was stumbling along a wall, waving his arms in a windmill fashion. He was using the wall to support himself and unfortunately coming along the wall was a blind girl in a big hurry. She was tapping on the wall and moving fast. The onlookers had seconds to react but no one did and the two students collided along that wall and fell in a tangle of arms and legs. No one laughed and all of us rushed to help untangle them. It was a pathetic sight but at the same time there was a pause to appreciate the courage of these two people in overcoming their problems and continuing to their classes.

The campus had many disabled students and we never knew if we should help them or not to navigate up some ramp. Did they want to be left alone or be helped by someone?

Not all things on campus where drinking and pranks. I tried to organize a branch of our fraternity on the campus. I wanted to start a Neo-Lithuania fraternity on campus for Lithuanians to get together. Most of the Lithuanian guys from Chicago already belonged to either the Catholic Ateitininkai or the scout Akademikai. I had to find a different Lithuanian pool of people to try to organize. I got the phone directory of the men's residence halls and started making calls to Lithuanian sounding names. It was a great experience in talking to DPs like me but I also encountered second and third generation guys that wanted to know more about their heritage. I invited all of them to meetings I had organized and we started some activities. Nothing much came of this because there was a fast turnover of people coming and going from the campus.

One interesting thing happened from this unification effort was that a good friend of mine, Romas, who had come from Australia got dragged into the Lithuanian vortex of activity and became a member of our fraternity Neo-Lithuania, married a great Lithuanian girl and raised a Lithuanian family.

I had mentioned earlier that the Lithuanians always seem to want to congregate, some sort of tribal instinct. My friends on campus were mostly all Lithuanian except for Bruce. Lithuanians had one thing that drew us together and that was drinking on weekends. The Lithuanians most of the time went to the Thunderbird beer hall while I favored a place called the Wigwam.

I mentioned a lot about the Urbana campus but nothing about some of the courses, what is with me and total disregard for education. I had some great courses and extremely intelligent teachers that truly challenged us. I really liked psychology and should have gotten a PHD in it, and gone on to Hollywood to become a shrink there and make millions, but that was not in the stars. I did earn almost a minor in psych, I had nineteen hours, you needed twenty.

The Psych teacher that I believed was so great was a Doctor Fishbein. He had authored a book on Social Psychology where he created a standard of measuring attitudes toward anybody or anything. Let us for example use the black person that we wanted to measure attitudes in a class toward him. We would first gather a belief list about black people such as, they are great athletes, they are great dancers, they are great singers, they are kind, they are dirty, they are stupid, they are inclined to crime, they are cruel and a bunch more. Now you would list all the beliefs and rate them on a one to ten basis, one being slight and ten being max, you would also use positive and negative numbers. The class would do the rating about a black person and you would have either negative or positive scores. You could now measure how different individuals feel about black people.

This idea could and is being used today as a propaganda tool to sell attitudes about anything. War, Gay people for example can be all painted with positive beliefs to change peoples attitudes. Doctor Fishbein invented a way to measure attitude and that to me was a great learning experience.

I also had some great journalism classes where the teachers actually brought in real Soviet communists to talk to us about the Soviet freedom of the press. This was so interesting to me to hear a real communist from the Soviet Embassy talk to us. I hated communism so badly but I was curious how a card carrying party member would defend their rotten system.

The man was a good speaker and he said things that made sense on the surface. He said once the scientists, professors decide on some issue and the party approves their decision why confuse the public with some conflicting ideas that would be presented by not so qualified people. If the real brain trust decides that 80% of the farms should grow corn why allow some unqualified person to write that they should grow wheat.

He went on to explain how we waste brain power in allowing advertising to push people from one brand to another. As an example he stated that we have so many different cigarettes and there are so many smart people wasting their time getting smokers to go from one brand to another. A waste of brain power hc said. In the Soviet Union experts sample and create the best tasting cigarette, one regular and one menthol and that is the end of it. All the advertising people can now get real productive jobs instead of wasting their time and brains on getting people to switch brands. This kind of made sense, but we did not buy it because we were studying marketing, advertising, news writing something that did not fit in the Soviet Union. It was good for us to hear how the dark side behaved.

One other class where we had a lot of laughs was the actual production of commercials. We had a project that we had been given about the introduction of the frozen pouch of vegetables for Green Giant. We had to start by investigating peoples attitude about what to call this pouch, Should we call it a bag, a sack, a pouch or what. What were the different connotations on different names? We settled after many surveys that pouch was alright and we now proceeded to film and produce a real commercial. We got a bunch of young kids to sit around a table eating the pouch cooked vegetables and then a large guy, dressed like the Green Giant would come through a door and ask the kids how they enjoyed the fast cooked, flavored vegetables. It seemed like a great commercial but we failed to understand that the film was in black and white and our ability to make the big guy look like the Green Giant was an impossibility. We had painted the guy green and added tons of squiggly paper strips to his jump suit. So . . . for our showing of our commercial we had a big lecture hall with the movie camera and had many of our professors attending to see the results of educating us in the advertising field. The commercial started really well and the kids looked happy and enjoyed eating the vegetables. Then the door opened and the Green Giant entered, the kids looked like they were surprised by this huge looking Frankenstein type guy who looked terrible with the bad makeup. The creature looked so bad that you could not hear what was being said because the audience was falling out of their chairs laughing. We had to laugh also because the giant ended up looking like a horror type creature. We ended up getting a mediocre grade because we had done a lot of research for marketing and the commercial was only a part of the grade. I do believe our group would have done better dancing dressed like different vegetables and then all of us jump into a plastic giant bag and show the people how happy, we, the vegetables, were to be bagged or pouched.

Many other events and incidents happened every day but the memorable ones, like memorable people, leave a very deep impression on the mind.

One such event occurred when I had to leave for Urbana after a semester break, and so, the Sunday before I left I went to a huge Lithuanian picnic. Lithuanians were known for their picnics. There was always a lot to drink, great food and a lot of friends to see. This Sunday I ran into a childhood friend, Richard, I knew him from Germany and then I would run into him at different Lithuanian functions. Richard and I enjoyed the picnic and I told him I had to take a train to Urbana the next day. Richard said that he could drive me to Urbana in his old Pontiac convertible, but he failed to mention that on that Monday he had to start a new job and had classes scheduled at some junior college. Richard already had a drinking problem then but I did not realize it.

We set out super early with my suitcases, books, because I had classes later on that day. We were close to Urbana when the car broke down and we rolled into a closed gas station. There we were, stranded in a one horse town. Lucky for us that a cop drove by and got suspicious of us sitting in a closed gas station. After we explained that we were on the way to Urbana and I showed him my student ID, we started looking at the engine. It seemed to us and the cop that the engine was blown. The cop said he would buy the car for parts and so we sold it to him for some small amount. It seemed strange to me that Richard acted so impulsively. So . . . here we were on the highway to

Urbana standing with all my stuff and hitchhiking. A farmer was kind enough to stop with his pickup truck and let us ride in the open back to the outskirts of Urbana where we were able to get a cab to my dorm, Snyder house.

I left Richard in my room and ran off to my Journalism class which was news writing or something like that. I sat down in the class and all of us had an ancient old typewriter in front of us. I thought we would have discussions on the freedom of the press, and such, but the teacher said insert some paper in the typewriter and write your autobiography.

I did not know how to type, adjust the typewriter so I pecked away with one finger. I do not know how I survived this. The only interesting thing that happened in that class was that I had Roger Ebert in that class and he later became very famous. I remember him as a skinny kid with a big mouth.

This whole prelude of my new semester now morphed into a complex situation where my mother kept calling me and Richard's mother called me. Richard did not want to go home to Chicago, he wanted to stay with me in Urbana.

During the day he slept in my room, I would sneak him into the cafeteria and grab extra food for myself and share it with Richard. In the evenings we would go out for beer and I introduced him to some of the girls I knew. Richard was good looking and soon he was going out with the girls and was having a great time. He had some money and so this type of life went for a while. I was becoming more confused at this relationship of ours and the mothers wanted to know why I would not send Richard home.

Finally Richard ran out of money. He could not go out on dates anymore. I believed my problem was over . . . but no, Richard had no bus fare to go to Chicago. I finally borrowed some money from friends and gave Richard the money for the bus. I arranged with a friend with a car to drive him to the bus stop. I firmly believed my crazy problem had ended. Not so, Richard now could date again using the bus money, so there he was back at my dorm.

The mothers kept calling me and I decided to try again to get some money together and this time buy him a ticket to Chicago. I did it right and put him on the bus. Richard and I hung around again in 1968 but I never realized he was an alcoholic and needed help so badly. I must have had my head up my ass not to be able to help this kind, good, friend, that needed help so desperately.

The next incident which today I consider ugly was funny at the time. I mentioned before I had friends coming from Chicago to visit and party with in Urbana. One time a group of about four guys came down on a Friday evening from Chicago. They wanted to go out with some college girls that evening. I was disciplinarian and knew the officers in the girls dorms so I called them and a friend of mine there was a social director. She rounded up about six or eight girls that had no dates that evening. My friends on the floor also wanted to go out so we figured out how many guys and how many girls would be going on this blind date. We had a big crowd now and somebody said that we could also have some secret fun by throwing five dollars in what is called a pig pool. The college had those games going on. It was that the guys on blind dates would judge who ended up with the worst date for the evening and would win all the money in the pig pool.

We went out to one of the big beer halls and had pizza and beer and joked around and flirted with the girls. The girls never knew they were being judged so cruelly. These girls were not the hotties who always had dates on Friday nights. The guys tried to point out to each other the faults of their dates. After we got back to the dorms the voting started as to who would win the pig pool. Arguments and presentations went on among the partially drunk guys until it was decided that so and so won the pig pool.

At that time I thought it was funny, today I think it was super cruel. These were fellow human entities wanting everything we all want, love, acceptance, recognition and we gave them shit, made fun of them. I would hope when they went back to their dorms they at least sat down and discussed what a bunch of ill behaved dveebs we were.

College might not bring you fame and money but it expands your vision about everything. Religion, politics, economics, history, science, and can all be seen in a more complete, correct, picture. Restraining chains on thinking that we are all brought up with are somewhat relaxed and we can see the world clearer which helps us navigate through it.

College also exposes you to many different people and makes your life more interesting. During my last two years in college I met a person that was very interesting, and entertaining, I am talking about Bruce who helped me with some of my disciplinarian duties. We played a lot of chess for those stay awake pills I always needed. I also enjoyed the rides in the Jaguar sports cars, the 140's and 150's, I believe.

I drove an Austin Healey Sprite right after graduation.

One time I took him to a party at Wally's house, a basement party. I introduced him to Wally and I said I want you guys to get to know each other because you are very similar, very special. I also used other words. I went on to say, in that basement doorway, in the early sixties, that there is some kind of aura about both of you and that I feel you will become either millionaires or end up in jail. I knew that somehow to be true at that time.

I ended up being right about both guys. Wally made his million dollars by living very correctly and Bruce became a multi millionaire by becoming an innovative, hard working industrialist with his own business.

Bruce never graduated from college, I believe he was, one hour short, and felt he did not need that piece of paper.

We somehow kept in touch over the next few years, and that I consider a great gift to me that we did not loose contact. We got together on rare occasions even thou we were traveling in different directions. I was working as a successful toilet paper salesman, driving around my area calling on stores. Bruce was meanwhile building a coating, Teflon, business in a ghetto type industrial area. I stopped in to see him a few times and it was interesting to hear his stories of the criminal attacks by blacks on his little factory and his defense attempts to protect his little kingdom.

He was always being broken in through a large window so he rigged a door on hinges above the window that was weighed down by bricks. The door had long nails hammered through it and was set to trip when the window was forced or broken. This to both of us was so funny to visualize the creepy animals crawling through the window, tripping it and then getting slammed in the head or body with the heavy door and nails.

There was also a flat roof where the animals would exit through another window with their loot. There was always water on this flat roof so Bruce rigged up an electric charge in the water. In the morning he would find his typewriter on the roof where the creeps were shocked by the electric charge. Fun was had by all except for the creeps.

Bruce today holds many patents but in those days he was the innovator. With a very limited budget the man built mechanical conveyors that sprayed the products, he was coating, and fed them through the ovens he built and incorporated in his system. When you saw this whole crude system in this decrepit old building you felt sorry for this hard working friend. He had his money problems, his criminal attack problems, his ventilation problems that were possibly affecting his health, but he overcame them all.

He is living proof that the American Dream can be had, but you need a superior brain, an iron will, and super creativity, if you do not have that then go work for someone or go become a politician.

I was working for four years, very short hours, for the paper product co. Charmin Paper division of P&G. I had the time to visit Bruce and have good conversations. I had a beautiful girlfriend, a company car, what else could a guy want, but I was a restless spirit and I started a vending machine business on the side, I soon had fifteen locations where I had gumball machines and nickel and dime toy machines. I was also a coin collector so I looked through the coins for rare dates.

Bruce and I met at different times but he had a road he picked out and was sticking to it while I still had a long way to go before I found my own road.

College gave us a better chance to succeed, opened more doors, introduced us to new friends, made us better people, and all this was done at an affordable cost to the student. That was a different world from today, all of us graduated with no debt, and had thousands of jobs to pick from. Today we have to give ourselves an answer as to what happened to our world? Who is to blame? We can try to explain that it is the fault of our incompetent, warmongering politicians, or is it no one's fault, it is simply globalization, overpopulation, competition for limited resources that have destroyed our opportunities to live the American Dream.